When Do I Start?

RICHARD FISCHER OLSON

WHEN DO I START?

• • •

A Nine-Point Strategy for Getting the Job You Want

WARNING:

This Book May Be Harmful to Interviewers!

Quill • William Morrow • New York

Grateful acknowledgment is made for permission to use the following:

The cartoon appearing on page 59: Reprinted with the special permission of Bo Brown.

The "Hagar the Horrible" cartoons appearing on pages 101, 109, and 231, and "The Lockhorns" cartoon appearing on page 107: Reprinted with the special permission of King Features Syndicate.

The cartoon appearing on page 156: Reprinted with the special permission of Tribune Media Services.

It is the policy of William Morrow and Company, Inc., and its imprints and affiliates, recognizing the importance of preserving what has been written, to print the books we publish on acid-free paper, and we exert our best efforts to that end.

Library of Congress Cataloging-in-Publication Data

Olson, Richard Fischer.
When do I start?: a nine-point strategy for getting the job you want / by Richard Fischer Olson.
   p. cm.
  Includes index.
  ISBN 0688-14073-4
  1. Employment interviewing. I. Title.
HF5549.5.I6039 1992
650.14—dc20
                                   91-48017
                                   CIP

Printed in the United States of America

First Quill Edition

1 2 3 4 5 6 7 8 9 10

BOOK DESIGN BY PATRICE FODERO

To Herbert John

For your support
your gentleness
your wonderlust for living

ACKNOWLEDGMENTS

• • •

Writing a book is a life event, one of thousands. It represents the sum total of comprehensions and apprehensions at a point in time. As such, it is not simply an act of researching and writing on a given topic. This book contains the influence of hundreds of people and experiences in my life, some not directly related to this activity and some I'm unaware of. But for those I can identify, I wish to publicly acknowledge my gratitude to:

My Stanford University stewardship which encouraged me to question the obvious, and especially the discussions with my colleagues Richard Carter, David Tronsgard and William Carey.

David Nierenberg and Bambe Levine for their confidence and willingness to introduce me to the literary community.

Al Zuckerman and the people at Writers House Inc. for their efforts in getting this book published.

Vice-president and editorial director Adrian Zackheim for his helpful suggestions and for putting up with my quirky and sometimes quixotic approach.

Editorial assistant Suzanne Oaks, who probably receives more work than credit (I understand that's part of an "assistant's" job description); copy editor Joan Marlow, who truly must be a saint or decidedly mad to so thoroughly and meticulously correct the accepted draft; Arlene Goldberg for coordinating the illustrations, cartoons and graphics; and Terry Guglielmino for drawing my leftfield sense of humor.

King Features of New York, Tribune Media Services in Chicago, and artist Bo Brown (Jenkintown, Pennsylvania) for granting permission to use their copyrighted cartoons. They are recognized wherever the cartoons appear in the book.

Eileen Sharaga and Stu Montal for reading and reacting to the manuscript.

And finally, I'm indebted to clients and colleagues who allow me to test ideas and applications, and provide feedback to guide future projects.

CONTENTS

. . .

A WORD TO THE READER

. . .

This is a job-getting book. Every route to employment goes through the interview.

This is a serious book. By applying its principles you should "pass" any interview.

This is a fun book. Some of my colleagues refer to it as the *"Barron's* of Interviewing."

This is an honest, hence irreverent and saucy book.

And, I believe, this is a needed book.

Needed because most treatises on the subject are written for interviewers or are "job-finding" books. I write for you— you who seek employment at all levels of society.

The few books directed at applicants tend to:

1. Emphasize what skilled interviewers do (I know only one.)

2. Tout interviewing as a cat-and-mouse game (It's not; it's shrewd business.)

3. Expound text principles and theories (versus usable tips)

4. Focus on pre-interview activities, e.g., finding job openings, writing résumés, completing applications

and correspondence and getting in the door (versus talking with employers)

I mean to say it as it is and on occasion even more than it is in an effort to pen an authentic full-color picture of what actually goes on face-to-face with prospective employers. I think too many of us treat the interview like the mystery of the Shroud of Turin. This book represents one effort to remove the veil, to get behind interviewers' behaviors and reveal intentions of which even they are unaware.

We all operate with biases, most of them unstated and many unformulated. It's important for me as an author to clarify the assumptions upon which this writing is based. You may choose to disagree, but at least you'll know my starting point.

Based on my knowledge, experience and preferences, I assume that

- The skills required to perform a job are not the same skills required to get the job.
- Most interviewers know diddly about what influences their decisions.
- Interviewing is not an honest process.
- Interviewing is not a rational process.

Scholars and managers have built a mythology around selection procedures. One part of the myth maintains that the interview is a good predictor of success on the job. True or false, little evidence supports this conclusion. In fact, the interview is far removed from the job. Both participants create an unreal world. Candidates paint showy self-portraits; interviewers submit truncated views of their organizations.

Someone once asked a Frenchman why France did not produce tennis players to match its wines. The answer was, "It is just because of our fine wines that we do not produce fine tennis players." The same query could be directed to personnel departments: "Why don't you select people to match your intricate employment system?" Answer: "It is because of our fine system that we do not select fine people."

All of this is written less to be critical than to be realistic. Anything else leaves us jousting with windmills. Why approach the interview like a "man overboard"? Why kamikaze your way through, bent on self-destruction? A strategy is in order, and that strategy should jibe with what is, not what ought to be.

Are all interviewers unaware? No. But the ones you will face are. Therefore take charge. Merchandise yourself. Position, display, color—the way you'd wrap a gift to impress someone special. Be an eye-catcher.

The primary purpose of this book is not to help you find openings—there are ample available sources for that.

This book will help you pass the interview, once you're in the door.

It outlines nine principles to follow for successful interviewing. If you understand these principles you will hold an edge over prospective employers. If you practice these principles you will get the job.

The ideas and recommendations here apply to all types of interviews, including screening by college recruiters, group sessions, stress situations, initial or final reviews. And they are equally relevant to varying backgrounds of interviewers, i.e., recruiters, headhunters, human-resource personnel, line managers or the actual supervisor for the job in question. That's because all your actions distill to one issue: Does the interviewer like you?

Recognize the facts. You want a job. You want to be hired,

promoted or transferred. You cannot trust that to the "expertise" of interviewers. You cannot continue to be awed by them, even if they act like gods. Placate them, yes. The interview is no time to stand on principle. Heresy leads to the gallows, so know the liturgy. As one of my Stanford mentors used to say, "What good is talent without a job?"

I set down recommendations as hypotheses, as are all truths. Try them. Raise the odds in your favor. More than half your waking life is devoted to work. Getting the right job is solely your responsibility. As long as the interview remains the critical factor in determining your vocational path, learn it well. Learn it better than the employer sitting across from you who will turn thumbs up or thumbs down on your application, on your career and ultimately on your life.

RFO

BEFORE

. . .

This interview is for a Marketing Assistant position with Metropolitan Products Inc. (MPI), a fictitious company. In the right-hand column I have added the interviewer's inner thoughts. You will be able to judge for yourself whether or not Pam got the job. Would you hire her?

Interview	Interviewer's Reactions
[*Pam, dressed in a baggy chartreuse blouse and red slacks, walks meekly into the room, looks at her shoes and offers a clammy handshake.*]	My God, what have I here, Little Miss Muffet?
INTERVIEWER: My name is Adrian, I'd rather go on that basis. Please sit down. What do you prefer to be called?	

Interview	Interviewer's Reactions
PAMELA: Ah . . . umm . . . Ms. Kensky.	
[*Long pause*]	Ms. Formality?
I: I notice you're an English major. Have you read Richardson much?	
P: Ah . . . umm . . . I read *Pamela*, of course.	
I: Did they require *Clarissa* also?	
P: No.	
I: Lucky you.	
[*Another pause*]	Ms. Talkative
I: Well, ah, what about our situation that particularly intrigued you, fascinated you?	
P: Umm . . . The job description, and it's close to home so I can take care of my cats.	The Cat Woman?
I: Without going into great detail, could you give me an ap-	

	Interview	**Interviewer's Reactions**
	preciation for what you do in a regular day from nine to five?	
P:	Umm . . . Well, I publicize books, primarily reviewed in professional journals. Ahh . . . I try to get author interviews or feature articles on the book.	
I:	How do you go about doing this sort of thing?	Puzzled
P:	Umm . . . By making up a mailing list for each of our books. Our books are rather specialized, so I make up an individual list for each one. And I also prepare a certain amount of publicity material.	
I:	Excuse me, does this mean press releases, blurbs, etc.?	Still puzzled
P:	Yes . . . yes . . .	

Interview	Interviewer's Reactions
[*Silence*]	I give up.
I: Okay, I'm going to go back into your past for a bit—I have a feel for what you're doing now. Tell me about yourself.	
P: Well . . . umm . . . there's not much to tell. What would you like to know?	
I: Well, why don't you start with schooling?	This is like pulling teeth.
P: Okay . . . umm . . . I graduated from Wellesley College	
I: Yes, I notice in English with high honors. Why English? What fascinated you about that, or was it simply the shortest line at registration?	
P: Actually . . . umm . . . I didn't like	

Interview	**Interviewer's Reactions**
any other subjects, plus my boyfriend was majoring in English.	
I: I see. . . . Let's address the time you've been with Felton, Inc., which is a little over two years. Are there one or two things you're most proud of? If someone asked you what you've contributed to the face of the earth over the last two years, other than the oxygen-CO_2 cycle, in your professional life, what would you answer to that?	No, I really don't.
P: Ah . . . umm . . . let's see. [*Pause*] Umm, I'm usually on time and mind my own business, and, right or wrong, do my job. That's it?	

	Interview	Interviewer's Reactions
I:	Hmm . . . What sort of things do you read on your own, other than books you have to write publicity about?	
P:	Umm . . . mysteries and romance novels.	
I:	Yes?	Some examples?

[*Silence*]

| | Where would you like to be going—I don't mean this as the usual inane question when people say, "Where do you want to be in five years?" No one really knows that. Where would you like to be going over the short haul, as it were? | |
| P: | Umm, I don't know. The future seems so far ahead. I guess I'd | |

	Interview	**Interviewer's Reactions**
	be content to stay here. . . .	
I:	Okay, I think you've answered the question. [*Pause*] Getting into a full-fledged marketing operation, there is a requirement for some statistical background. There's nothing in your experience that indicates you could cope with a large quantity of numbers. Have you had any exposure to this sort of thing?	No objectives, no plan, no aspirations
P:	Umm, not really. I was never very good at math in school. But I can balance my checkbook.	
I:	Okay . . . [*Another pause*] Uh-huh . . . Well, the job is not that heavily statistically oriented, but there	Hmmm . . . ?

	Interview	Interviewer's Reactions
	is some of it in there. . . .	
	In your present position you have some supervisory responsibility. How many people are you supervising now?	
P:	Umm . . . My position is more coordination and liaison, but I have an assistant and half a clerk.	
I:	Hmm, half a clerk, that must be tricky.	
P:	Well, umm, you see, she also works half time for someone else.	
I:	Yes, of course . . . How do you get them to do the things that need to be done?	I guess it wasn't so funny.
P:	Umm, I just tell them.	
I:	Okay . . . What would you say, if you had to catalog	I wish it were that easy.

	Interview	**Interviewer's Reactions**
	your virtues, are your strongest points?	
P:	Umm . . . I'm punctual, I like working with people . . . umm . . .	
I:	Uh-huh . . . If you had to fall back on one or two skills to accomplish your business objectives, what would they be?	Be more specific, dammit.
P:	I guess that's it . . . umm . . . punctuality and working with people.	
I:	Okay, good. There is one more question I would want to ask you. If you had the entire realm of recorded history to choose from, whom would you want to spend a day with?	I guess that *is* it.
P:	Ah . . . umm . . . Gee, that's a tough one. Umm . . . I don't know . . .	

Interview	Interviewer's Reactions
maybe Madonna or Dolly Parton . . . or, umm . . .	

[*Pause*] Rather shallow

I: Okay, that's about all the questions I have. Do you want to ask me anything about the job or MPI?

P: Umm . . . No, I can't think of anything.

[*Pause . . . Adrian stands up*] Not very discerning, unprepared

Umm . . . what happens now?

I: This has been an interesting interview. Of course, I have a number of other candidates to see. A lie

[*As they reach the door . . . pause*]

Interview	**Interviewer's Reactions**
I: Thanks for coming. Oh, by the way—Don't call us, we'll call you!	Reject.

Part One

. . .

STATE OF THE ART: MYTHS ABOUT INTERVIEWING

. . .

This section examines the state of the art, emphasizing the gap between what interviewers say and what they actually do. Questions that are answered include:

- Do interviewers know what they're doing?
- What is interviewing?
- What are standard interviewing procedures?
- How do interviewers prepare?
- What do interviewers look for?
- Are interviews reliable?
- Are they valid?
- How important are job qualifications?
- What influences interviewers most?

MYTHS ABOUT INTERVIEWING

. . .

. . .

> Interviewing is more feeling
> and gut reaction than logic and reason.

. . .

"Matchmaker, matchmaker, make me a match, . . ." sing the daughters in the 1964 Broadway musical *Fiddler on the Roof*. Of course, they are referring to marriage. This book concerns a merger of another kind—finding a job to suit your skills, talents and interests. And for that there is no Yente, no "little ol' matchmaker" with whom to supplicate. Other than the scattered advice you may be given by a few authors, placement specialists and friends, you are left to your own devices.

Three out of four persons are not taxing their potential and do not feel fulfilled by their work. If you are one of those, if you are without a job or want to change vocations, if you seek a promotion or transfer to some activity that allows for creative as well as routine skills—this book is for you.

Take on matchmaking for yourself. Sure it's scary, but don't be overwhelmed. Batten up your uncertain hatches, cast aside your slugabed approach, and with me jump into the muscle of this figmental monster called the Interview.

What Is It?

You are graduating from school and looking for your first job.

You are bored and want something more stimulating.

Your company is cutting back and eliminating your department.

You've just been fired.

You want to move up to greater responsibility and more money.

You're looking for a job.

This is what you're facing:

- An economic decline
- Increasing foreign competition
- Companies cutting staff
- An increase in the number of candidates for the best jobs

It's a jungle out there. You beat the pavement, read want ads, send letters and résumés, sweat and pray. Then finally, an invitation to interview, and you start talking to yourself:

Now what? How should I prepare? What should I wear? What do I say about myself? What are they going to ask me? What happens if I draw a blank? I can't think, I can't think. How do I hide my ner-

vousness? I don't have much experience. And my grades in school, what will they think of them? Oh, God, I got a pimple on my chin. What if I fall flat on my face? I can't face it. I don't know if I can do it. I'll never get a job.

True, the interview can be a harrowing experience. It is a plague sometimes, a molestation of sorts that must be endured. But until legislated a crime or upgraded to a modestly rational level, it is a necessity to be mastered.

For organizations the interview is the car wash of employment, caravanning bodies in hopes of emerging with one sparkling one. It's a sedative in the medicine kit of employment practices, dulling fear of failure and providing a false sense of surety. Most managers approach it like Pin the Tail on the Donkey, hoping that with one stroke of luck they will tack people in the proper place.

No matter what you call it, an interview has the following elements:

- Two or more persons
- An exchange of information, verbal and nonverbal
- Feelings
- A decision

This process constitutes the single most important hiring technique, bar none. "Do not hire without a face-to-face interview" has become a management axiom. As if truth is in seeing, and we all know "seeing is believing." [1]

Standard procedures for employment include:

[1] I suspect the outcome of human events is more likely determined by "I'll see it when I believe it."

1. An application
2. A screening interview, usually thirty minutes in length, conducted by a recruiter in a small office on campus, a hotel, or in the organization's personnel department
3. An interview with the boss or department head
4. The hiring discussion in which details of salary, benefits, medical examination and starting time are formalized

"Want to catch the 3:00 executions in the Personnel Tower?"

Of course these four steps vary according to level of responsibility. For lower-paying jobs a fifteen-minute discussion might constitute the entire routine. With most positions, though, expect at least two interviews.

The employment system is fraught with mythology and misunderstanding. This book raises some serious questions about the whole process:

- Do interviewers know what they're doing?
- How do they go about gathering information?
- Are their decisions logical and rational?
- Are there unseen factors that play a part in whether or not you are hired?
- Do the most qualified usually get the job?

Answering these questions leads to an exploration of a number of myths about interviewing. By "myth" I mean a belief unsubstantiated by everyday events. The eleven myths below refer to interviewing as normally conducted, not as interviewers say, or as textbooks write, it should be.

Myth #1: Interviewers Prepare.

On the contrary, most interviewers don't even know your name. Nor do they read your résumé, except maybe two minutes before the appointment.

Scenario

SECRETARY: "Ms. Kensky is here."
INTERVIEWER: "Who's that?"

S:	"The applicant you asked to come in about the marketing assistant's job."
I:	"Ah, um, where's her application?"
S:	"There in your In-basket. Remember, I gave it to you last Monday?"
I:	"Oh, yes. Have her wait until I get a chance to look at it."

In addition to this too-often-true script, interviewers keep skimpy records during and immediately after the session. Since memories fade fast, the longer the wait, the more they forget. The implications of inadequate preparation and record-keeping are explored in Part Two.

Myth #2: If Two or More Managers Interview You, They Will Come up with the Same Recommendation.

Interviews are notoriously unreliable, much like the classroom. A student can do the same quantity and quality of work, yet receive an "A" from one teacher and a "C" from another. Teachers differ in their concept of what constitutes an "A" versus a "C." Interviewers demonstrate this same "range of acceptability." They vary markedly in their ratings on the same set of criteria for the same candidate.

Scenario

| INTERVIEWER 1: | "I thought Ms. Bergeson was too aggressive, too pushy. She'll be difficult to manage." |
| INTERVIEWER 2: | "On the contrary, we need that kind of drive. I like her energy. She knows how to get a job done." |

INTERVIEWER 3:   "Hey, I think you're both missing the point.
                 The woman just doesn't have enough ex-
                 perience."
VICE PRESIDENT: "Are you sure the three of you interviewed
                 the same applicant?"

Myth #3: Interviewing Is an Important Activity in Organizational Life.

Nonsense. As a management function interviewing is ig-
nored. Yes, organizations give lip service to the importance
of hiring competent people, but most managers have not had
one day of how-to training. If anything, the norm is to include
a module on interviewing, usually one to two hours, as part
of general management development. In reading this book you
will surpass most recruiters' education on the dynamics and
techniques of interviewing.

Myth #4: Interviewers Understand the Job for Which You Are Applying.

Not usually, especially in the first interview. Most have not
worked in the positions they advertise. Take a secretary. It's
rare for interviewers to talk to the boss to find out what he
or she really needs and looks for in a secretary. With technical
areas such as research, engineering and manufacturing, the
vagaries are more pronounced. Before meeting you, few interviewers search out answers to:

1. What are the five major responsibilities of the job, in order of priority?

2. How do superstars in that position carry out those responsibilities?

3. What are the technical requirements?

4. What problem-solving skills are needed?

5. What are the "getting along with people" demands?

The implication is, since interviewers tend to be unfamiliar with the demands of the specific position, they will choose you for reasons other than your fitness for the job.

Myth #5: Interviewers Are Objective.

Objectivity is a desired state never achieved. We all have notions, fixed by our backgrounds and experience, which we bring to every human activity. We are influenced by the extraneous as well as the relevant. For instance, I am partial to left-handers, grass-court tennis, simplicity, Scandinavian design, opera, entrepreneurship, woodlands, scuba diving, the wind, open-endedness, Robert Frost, hard work and diversity. Most likely I would hire a Swedish southpaw tennis player who writes poetry and enjoys the ocean, classical music and fireplaces.

The most interviewers can hope for is awareness of biases and, on occasion, a temporary detachment from them. I estimate that on the ten-point scale below interviewers operate at a "3" or "4" level.

Subjective   Objective
```
 |____._____.__X__.____.____.____.____.____.__|
   1    2    3    4    5    6    7    8    9    10
```

Myth #6: Interviewers Listen.

They talk. In a videotape study I found that most inter-viewers estimate they speak one fourth of the time and listen three fourths. Instant replay substantiated the opposite: They talk through 75 percent of the interview. Sad state of affairs for someone who's supposed to search for data upon which to base an important decision. Plus, the remaining 25 percent does not ensure listening time, only that interviewers aren't opening their mouths. They could well be thinking of the next question to ask.

(These findings trigger an interesting hypothesis: The more you can get interviewers to talk, the more likely you will be hired.)

Myth #7: Interviewers Look for Individuality and Uniqueness in Candidates.

The truth is, interviewers seek conformity. They tend to hire in the image of themselves and the organization. Research suggests that interviewers feel more "at home" with applicants who exhibit similar interests, lifestyles and beliefs.

Most recommendations to hire include a justification to the effect that "Ms. Ploumis would make a fine addition to the department. She is cooperative and fits in well with our team— the kind of employee MPI would be proud of."

Myth #8: Honesty Is the Best Policy.

A lie. As we shall see in Principle 4, honesty may be a noble moral goal, but it will not necessarily get you the job.

Scenario

INTERVIEWER: "Why do you want to leave your current position?"

APPLICANT: "Well, to be honest, my boss is a very difficult person to work for. He's too demanding, too critical."

INTERVIEWER: "I see." (To herself: "A potential malcontent. If he were on *The Gong Show*, I'd be reaching for the rubber mallet about now.")

Myth #9: Interviewers Attempt to Find Out Your Strengths.

Actually, they ferret out weaknesses, infirmities, behaviors that disqualify. Above all, interviewers don't want to look bad. Overlooking capable candidates provides no embarrassment because colleagues never know how many good ones get away. But select a goldbricker, one bimbat and the interviewer's own job is in jeopardy.

In a way interviewers are like art and music critics. They wouldn't be doing their job if they didn't find something wrong.

Myth #10: Interviewers Wait Until All Information Is Gathered Before They Decide to Hire or Not Hire.

On the contrary, most decisions to accept or reject are made in the first minutes. The rest of the session is conducted to substantiate that decision. In interviewing, as in many interpersonal situations, first impressions persist. Principle 2 debunks the myth and spells out what to do about it.

Myth #11: Interviewers Hire or Recommend Applicants with the Best Job Qualifications.

Sometimes, maybe, but not usually. Interviews consist of an ebb and flow of emotions between two people, only occasionally interrupted by a fact. Feelings take precedent. Seldom do job factors alter a dislike of an applicant. Likableness comes first, job qualifications second.

Recognize these myths and take them into account. Organize yourself for what is, not what ought to be.

To ignore them is to miss the target. Your performance will be 180 degrees from what it takes to succeed.

To ignore them is job suicide.

.   .   .

Interviewing skills are not
the same as job skills.

.   .   .

What Do Interviewers Look For?

When three hundred interviewers were asked what they could determine about an applicant in the interview, they cited the following qualities:

aggressiveness

tough-mindedness

missing information

ability to see the broad
    picture

sense of humor

ability to inspire others

energy level

dynamic personality

verbal expression

analytical mind

quality of judgment

interests and hobbies

friendliness and warmth

professionalism

sincerity

career aspirations

commitment

courage

willingness to accept criticism

physical appearance

intelligence

honesty

work ethic

self-confidence

organization

literacy

creative spirit

decisiveness

enthusiasm

perseverance

background

philosophy and goals

record of job performance

good upbringing

**reason for choosing "our"
    organization**

cooperativeness

humility

attitude

**ability to appraise strengths
    and weaknesses**

poise under pressure

loyalty

problem-solving ability

maturity

At best only one fourth of the items on the list (indicated in boldface) represent behaviors that occur in a 30-to-60-minute interview. For instance background, job performance, problem-solving, commitment, accepting criticism, cooperation and poise under pressure could better be assessed by examining the candidate's past education and experience and talking to former employers or associates.

Judging sincerity, humility, loyalty, intelligence, honesty, warmth and the like requires a larger sample of behavior than that provided by the interview.

Enthusiasm, energy level and sense of humor are borderline. The stress of an interview may mute those traits, yet in more natural settings an applicant might exhibit them in abundance.

My conclusion is that interviewers look for many qualities and characteristics not observable during an interview.

If that is the state of things, you must prepare accordingly. Present yourself in a manner fitting and in consonance with that state. If this sounds Machiavellian, so be it. To do more or less would be subversion and stupidity.

.   .   .

> When a customer asks for a double-dip cone,
> don't waste time selling a single dip.

.   .   .

Nothing takes the place of competence on the job, but that can be acquired. Experience shows we learn more about a particular job in the first six months in the position than in all our schooling combined. Right now, you must first make a choice: become proficient at interviewing. If you succeed at that, you'll have ample opportunity to demonstrate expertise in your occupation.

This book concentrates on positioning the interviewer between your talents and the demands of the job, and on developing a self-concept that says, "I know what I'm doing... I'm the right person for this position." Skill and style, substance and spirit. That's what I'm talking about.

If you're looking for a job, this is a timely walk-through series of techniques. I hope I can convey a sense, a touch, for interviewing, so that what you learn and do will be a part of you, will be natural and spontaneous and believable.

Pull yourself out of interviewing doldrums. Set your sights high, then develop the necessary tools to substantiate those expectations. "It's a sad oarsman who learns to paddle when going over the falls." Now is the time to master the mechanics, so when you sit down in that chair, you, not the interviewer, hold the edge.

Proficiency does not come naturally. It requires digging and practice (you knew there would be a catch to it somewhere), but the payoff can mean a difference in the quality of your life.

Beethoven was known to form a complete symphony in his head before he composed. During the last three decades of his life he jotted ideas in a sketchbook. By the time he was ready to write the first movement of a symphony, all he had to do was transpose key elements from his notes. *When Do I Start?* can be your sketchbook for interviewing. This tapestry of ideas interwoven with your own should prepare you for the expected and unexpected.[2] The resulting blend will be a function of both of us, with your unique touch.

Take your career in your own hands. Don't be an inter-

---

[2]Though they start from an outline or structure, artists admit that unanticipated creativity emerges as different elements are manipulated. Expect the same phenomenon in interviewing. Knowledge and preparation will make it possible for you to respond to surprises in new and wondrous ways.

viewee cripple, wheelchaired to the myth that interviewers know so much more than you. Employment is their precinct, but that doesn't mean they're familiar with the environment.

The Paleolithic state of the art assures us that we need not approach the sanctuary with head bowed. Learn the music as well as the words. Understand the myths and make them work for you.

Getting a job is as complex as doing it. There are no bromides to wash away your anxiety. So get to it. Time is short, and we have much to cover before you feel comfortable and competent.

TIPS

Develop a realistic mind-set toward interviewing by remembering that, generally:

- Interviewers do not prepare.
- Interviews are unreliable.
- Interviewing is not treated as an important organizational activity.
- Interviewers do not understand the jobs they are trying to fill.
- Interviewing is a subjective event.
- Interviewers do not listen.
- Interviewers do not look for individuality.
- Honesty is not the best policy.
- Interviewers search out weakness, not strength.
- Interviewers make decisions with scant information.
- Results of interviews are not based on job qualifications.

A NOTE ON TIPS: Throughout the book I try to link concepts to actual interviewing. This linkage takes the form of workable recommendations. I refer to these as TIPS (Theory Into Practice Suggestions). Any one taken separately may seem oversimplified or rinky-dink. The intent is not to hang on one technique. Instead I offer a gallimaufry of ideas, which you must sort through and adapt to your style and concerns.

Part Two

. . .

PRINCIPLES FOR "PASSING" THE INTERVIEW

. . .

The interview is a test, more momentous than any college exam. You must pass with flying colors or you won't pass at all. This section tells you how to cram for that final.

I set forth nine principles that form the base for a strategy to enhance your chances. Some of the questions discussed are:

- How do you get your foot in the door?
- Is homework really necessary?
- How do you position yourself for a particular job?
- What is an interplan?
- What do you do for openers?
- How do you create an immediate positive impression?

- How do you determine the interviewer's likes and dislikes?
- Should you take a stand on issues?
- Should you ever be dishonest?
- Do you talk about deficiencies in your performance?
- How important is how you say it versus what you say?
- What about flair and aggressiveness—where do they fit in?
- Can you control outcomes in an interview?
- How do you press the interviewer's hot button?
- What's the best way to close?
- Is there a formula for success?

PRINCIPLE 1. ENTRY AS AN ALIEN

. . .

Chance favors only the mind that is prepared.

—*Louis Pasteur*

Despite changing lifestyles, work is still a major part of the American ethic. Whether for survival or fulfillment we work, work, work. Every individual, every organization, every nation needs an economic base from which to operate. Employment stands for money, and money buys time—time to develop talent, find a place and pursue activities that bring joy and satisfaction. Unless you have the proverbial rich uncle or choose a life of crime, the need for money requires a job. Personally, I have tried alternatives but always end up returning to work.

Except in cases of internal promotion, seeking employment means we enter as outsiders, as aliens. Typically we do not know the language, the customs and rituals. We are disadvantaged because we lack insider information and are viewed with suspicion by the natives. Being an alien can be a fearsome challenge, as my family, who immigrated through Ellis Island, would attest.

This chapter deals with two aspects of entry:[3]

A.   Getting In

B.   Doing Your Homework

Photo credit: Ibrahim Bullo

[3]Since I have chosen to concentrate on interviewing as a *job-getting* process, this chapter is a skimmer. For *job-hunting* starters, try Robert Bolles's durable *What Color Is Your Parachute?* (Berkeley, California: Ten Speed Press, 1972, and revised 1991).

A. Getting In

Getting in is not a "catching out" routine, where so-called "casual workers" wait on street corners for someone to come along and randomly assign jobs for the day. Getting in is a diabolically planned process.

You can obtain an interview in two ways:

1. Know Someone
2. Other

There is no substitute for insider help. The effectiveness of all other approaches wouldn't fill a thimble.

1. Know Someone

Except for positions filled through college recruiting, most jobs are obtained in informal ways through people contacts rather than agencies, classified ads or cold calls. The first step: Inventory friends and acquaintances. Make a complete list of those in your inner and outer social circles. Don't be surprised if you come up with a hundred or more names.

Talk to each one about your aims and objectives. They may pinpoint openings that fit your experience and aspirations or refer you to other sources. In addition to this list of potential helpers, introduce yourself at social gatherings, at church and at other group meetings. Don't be shy.

·   ·   ·

> Opportunity presents itself to the bold.

·   ·   ·

This is a "link age." Forge a human chain, each individual linked to another and another and another. You need names, so when you call or write about employment you can say, "Charlie Radken suggested I contact you."

One Caveat: You're not asking for a recommendation. People are hesitant to help because they're afraid it will be construed as an endorsement. Should you fall on your keester, they look bad.

Entering as an alien through a "familiar face" is the approach of choice. What are some other options?

2. Other

Employment Agencies and Executive Recruiters

Depending on the position, these vary in their effectiveness but certainly are a resource. You can find them easily enough in the Yellow Pages. The fee can be passed on to employers. Keep in mind that agencies are in the business of selling applicants. You cannot always rely on them to act in your best interest.

College Placement Bureaus

An obvious source if you are a college graduate. Placement officials will alert you to corporate interviewing schedules.

Telephone

Select organizations you're interested in, call the switchboard and ask who the personnel manager is, or sales manager or department head. Normally they give out these names quite freely. Call that person directly.

This is tough duty, with high probability you won't get

through. To enhance your chances don't act like an alien. Try: "Hi, this is Joleen, may I speak to Mr. Robertson, please?" Most secretaries will assume by your tone that you know Robertson. Unless asked directly, don't reveal your purpose, or you'll be cut short, shuttled to another office or told to send in a résumé.

Job-Finding Clubs

Supposedly the original club was founded in Carbondale, Illinois. Check for one in your area. Members share job leads, review each other's résumés, criticize interviewing styles and provide encouragement. Of the original sixty members who faithfully attended Carbondale Club meetings, 90 percent were working within two months.

Forty-Plus Clubs

In metropolitan areas such as New York, Chicago, Phila-delphia, Denver, Houston, Los Angeles and Honolulu, do-it-yourself help groups have organized for the over-forty crowd. Concentrating on managerial and white-collar positions, they offer refuge for employees with no golden parachute or union hall. Members participate in group therapy sessions, receive tips on résumés, access a file on job openings and even share outplacement consultations.

Outplacement Firms[4]

These differ somewhat from recruitment agencies. Con-tracted by companies as well as individuals, outplacement

[4]Going out of fashion is in-house outplacement known as the "Aloha Suite," an isolated office set aside by corporations for dismissed personnel where they can dictate correspondence, telephone prospects and generally stay out of the way.

firms emphasize job guidance. They help discharged persons deal with unemployment shock, self-appraisals, résumés and job-finding.

Jobathons

Coast-to-coast TV stations program "job fairs" where openings are solicited from area employers, and job seekers appear on the air. At this writing some three dozen stations have donated prime time to generate over twenty thousand jobs. Keep your eye on the TV listings and should a Jobathon come your way, participate.

Electronic Résumés

A few companies produce five-minute videotaped presentations of applicants that are distributed to prospective employers. Two drawbacks of this procedure:

1. Personnel departments don't always have video playback equipment located conveniently in offices where the videos are likely to be used.

2. Video can eliminate less photogenic candidates or those who do not come across well on the tube.

Computerized Job-Matching

Another kind of employment company computerizes photographs, résumés, salary requirements and other information to which subscribing employers have instant access. In Washington, D.C., alone, government computers now catalog more than eight thousand applicants for entry-level positions.

Skeptics claim the computer treats applicants as pieces of inventory. In some cases they find themselves matched to geographic areas in which they would not locate.

It looks like computer job-matching's time has come, and if you can afford the fee, test it out.[5]

Classified Ads

In an experiment with the Illinois State Employment Service, advertisements were placed in a local newspaper offering rewards for information about job openings. Informers were paid $100—$25 at the time the applicant was hired, plus three additional checks of $25 at the end of each week of the first three weeks of successful employment. The reward procedure resulted in ten times as many job leads and eight times as many placements as the standard practice.

If financially feasible, you might want to use some form of incentive system. Be inventive.

Correspondence

When you initiate a letter of application, send it to a specific person, not a department.

When canvassing "want ads," try to hide your astonishment when they don't acknowledge or you receive a "Dear John" response. That's common. Get used to "bell letters" that signal

---

[5]In cases of third-party assistance in finding a job, I recommend you do not pay an up-front fee. Most major cities list numerous examples of fraudulent agencies asking for one hundred dollars or more, then not delivering service. If an employment firm does not bill employers, insist that you pay upon performance.

the end of the round. Rejection is the norm. So, on to the next round and the next and the next. The fight has just begun.
Which brings us back to our "getting in" theme:

·   ·   ·

Writing to a box number is no match for face-to-face associations.

·   ·   ·

B. Doing Your Homework

Job junkets don't exist, unless your father owns the company (then, of course, you wouldn't be reading this book). Job-getting is tough business. You have to muck it out. How? *By preparating.*[6] That includes:

1.   Searching
2.   Shaping
3.   Simulating

---

[6]In Lewis Carroll's *Through the Looking Glass* Humpty Dumpty explains to Alice, "When *I* use a word, it means just what I choose it to mean—neither more nor less." He continues by defining the word *slithy*: "*Slithy* means 'lithe and slimy'. . . . You see it's like a portmanteau—there are two meanings packed up into one word." *Preparating* is my portmanteau word, a cross between prepping (cramming for the short haul) and preparing (planning long term).

1. Searching

Search the Organization

Use your local library to look up references to corporations. Try encyclopedias, stock market reports, the annual Dun & Bradstreet *Million Dollar Directory*, *Standard and Poor's Register of Corporations, Directors and Executives, Moody's Industrial Manual, National Business Employment Weekly* (Dow Jones) and Yeoman's *Job Annuals* (Putnam Press).

Write or visit the organization's headquarters to obtain a job description, PR publications, annual report, and other literature that will arm you with background information.

Visit places and interview people where the product is sold or service used. When possible, purchase the product or service. Try it out.

Entering the organization as an alien doesn't mean you have to be ignorant about its operation. Generally interviewers do not know the history of their own corporations. With a little digging, you will surpass their awareness.

Search Yourself

One reason not to fear interviews is that you're an expert on the topic being discussed: *you*. Snowflakes do not corner uniqueness. You have no clone. No one knows as much about you as you. Rummage through your experience and pick out activities and events that best present you.

Here are some ways to develop a presentation of self:

a. Write a brief autobiography. Not an easy task. Writing will force you to think through where you've been,

where you are and what got you there. To get you
started, reflect on the following:
- Early experiences that helped mold you
- Family history
- Significant school happenings
- Important work experiences
- Humorous incidents in your life
- Obstacles you overcame
- What you value
- People who have influenced you
- Travel adventures
- Hobbies and leisure interests
- Unusual accomplishments

b.   Imagine where you would like to be in 5 to 10 years,
     what you will be doing and with whom. Then define
     your goals, personal and professional. Knowing where
     you want to go makes it easier to determine how to get
     there.

c.   List strengths and weaknesses (ask friends for input)
     to gain a clearer picture of what you bring to the em-
     ployment table.

d.   If a job description is available, match your strengths
     to stated requirements. Specifically spell out the knowl-
     edge and skills in technology, problem-solving and in-
     terpersonal relations that relate directly to the job.
     Even without foreknowledge, be prepared to do this
     exercise as the job unfolds in the interview.

e.   List what you do well and don't do well, things you
     enjoy and don't enjoy about work. You may be asked
     for this kind of information.

NOTE: Of course, weaknesses and lack of skills are for your
analysis only. You cannot really understand yourself without

defining your limitations. Subsequent chapters spell out what information is safe for interviewers' ears.

2. Shaping

The Résumé

A résumé is a summing up, not a life history. Keep it short. Employers don't read. Condense and highlight. Omit dates. They give clues to age and may keep you out of the interview. If relevant, a chronology can be supplied in subsequent correspondence and meetings.

There's an old saying in college admissions: "The thicker the folder, the thicker the student." Add to that: "The longer the résumé, the longer you wait for a reply."

On the next page is a suggestive outline for your convenience. Include a cover letter that attempts to "hook" the reader with an unusual accomplishment, goal or interest. For instance:

- "I've been working on a technique for selling retailers that seems promising."
- "I have what I think are some effective cost-cutting ideas."
- "My goal is to become the most inventive engineer in the industry."

References

Don't hesitate to ask for letters of recommendation. They come with the territory. It's rare that anyone says something negative. They probably won't do much good or harm, but they may be expected.

Simple Outline for Your Résumé

Name_____

Address_____

Telephone_____

Job Objectives:

What are you looking for now?

What are your career aspirations?

Job Accomplishments:

What are you proud of?

What stands out in your personal and professional life?

What recognition and awards have you earned?

What would catch the employer's eye?

Job Experience:

What positions and organizations?

Education:

What schools, degrees, honors, areas of study?

References: (optional)

2 personal and 2 professional. (NOTE: Only supply these on request or if the names will influence employers to interview you.)

Richard Friedman, associate professor of medicine at the University of Wisconsin Medical School, laments that no one is ever poor, fair or average. In the fantasyland of recommendations, all are excellent or outstanding. He concludes that a dean's letter on Adolf Hitler might refer to him as "a natural leader, good at communications, assisted in the development of a number of technical advancements, did independent work with minority groups, likes to find solutions to problems and has a special interest in mental health."

Reprinted with special permission of Bo Brown.

"About the previous positions you've listed on your résumé—rich man, poor man, beggarman, thief, doctor, lawyer, merchant, chief—"

Be prepared to deliver your references *only if requested*, unless, of course, you have one from the President of the United States or some other notable.

An Interplan

Tennis, a harmless vanity of mine, has taught me that to succeed you must determine your opponent's strengths and weaknesses early on, then develop a strategy for winning (e.g., take the net, stay back, lob, hit to the backhand).

Anyone hearing General Norman Schwarzkopf's briefing at the end of the Gulf War had to be impressed, even breathless, at the thoroughness of the operation. Its planners could have been easily defeated by the enormity of the task of coordinating U.S. and allied air, naval and ground forces to defeat Iraq. Victory demanded analysis of allied and Iraqi capabilities, a design to fit the different elements together, competent execution and shrewd timing.

As in tennis and war, success in interviewing demands premeditation. I suggest an *interplan* (another "portmanteau") for moving your forces into the most advantageous position. It involves interlocking the best in you with requirements of the job and interviewer interests.

On the next page is an outline for an interplan.

For typical interviewer questions you should anticipate (III and IV of the interplan), see Appendix B.

Examples of questions to ask interviewers (V) appear under Principle 8 (page 182) and Principle 9 (page 199).

Timing

When to schedule an interview? Granted, you don't have total control over this, but usually you have some choice.

Outline for an Interplan

I. Pre-Interview Notes
  1. Correspondence
  2. Telephone
  3. Facts I Know
     • About the Organization
     • About the Job
II. Openers
  1. To Create Cordiality
  2. To Impress
III. Anticipated Questions About Me
  1. Interests
  2. Aspirations
  3. Strengths
  4. Limitations
IV. Anticipated Questions Related to the Job
  1. Experience
  2. Educational Background
  3. Accomplishments
  4. Other
V. Questions I Want to Ask
  1. About the Job
  2. About the Organization
  3. About Compensation and Career
VI. Wrap-up
  One Thing I Want the Interviewer to Remember

In a Robert Half study, the candidate interviewed last was hired 56 percent of the time, while the first applicant succeeded only 17 percent of the time. Perhaps interviewers heed the baseball adage about never hitting the first ball pitched. Since the Half interviewers talked with two to six persons in succession, one explanation might be that they were unable to recall earlier applicants. Or some interviewers gain insights as they go and ask more thoughtful questions, giving latecomers a better chance to shine.

ADVICE: In serial interviewing (college screening, for instance), avoid being one of the first applicants. Avoid immediately after lunch and late afternoon when people's energy levels are down.

3. Simulating

How do you get to Carnegie Hall?
Everybody knows: Practice, practice, practice.
Why practice?
To learn how to use prepared information in effective and appropriate ways.
Short of actual interviews, the best practice is simulation, in which you set up conditions to duplicate the real world.
How do you simulate?

1. Pick a friend or someone who, like yourself, is job-hunting. Ask him or her to play the interviewer.

2. Define a position you're interested in.

3. Interview for the job. The other person can use the most often asked questions listed in Appendix B.

4. Record the practice, so you have a sample of your interviewing performance to analyze and improve

upon. Videotape prepping is becoming popular on college campuses. You need to hear and see yourself. Bobby Burns wrote:

"Oh wad some power the giftie gie us
To see oursels as others see us!"

Sony has that power, and the gift is a VCR with instant replay.

5. Analyze and evaluate the interview with your colleague. (Use the evaluation form in Part Three.)

6. Make a list of things you do well in the interview, and techniques and skills you want to develop. Work on those in subsequent videotape practices.

NOTE: If you don't have access to video equipment, use audiotape. If no audio recorder, then ask a third person to observe and critique (again using the evaluation form in Part Three).

So *search, shape, simulate*. Crowbar your way in, because then and only then will you be in position to persuade an employer of your capabilities.

Use the checklist on the next two pages to aid in your preparation for a smooth entry.

"Preparating" for entrance as an alien is like cleaning out a closet. In the process you notice new things and discard paraphernalia no longer useful.

Now fortified, you're ready for a screen test. The medley in this chapter should convince you that the interview is not like a slot machine where you put in a quarter and pray. Though we are aliens, we minimize chance through foreknowledge.

Pre-Interview Checklist

I. Linkage	Names	Date	Disposition
____ People called			
____ People talked to			
____ Employment agencies			
____ Correspondence			
____ References			

II. Prospective Employer Information	Notes
____ Key employees (names)	
____ Job description (key responsibilities)	
____ Products & services	
____ Locations	
____ Financial information	
____ Competitors	

III. Personal Inventory	Notes
____ Résumé	
____ Dress	
____ Strengths (for convenience, write on 3 × 5 cards)	
____ Answers to anticipated questions (3 × 5 cards)	
____ Questions to ask	

IV. Scheduled Interviews	Date	Evaluation	Follow-up
____1.			
____2.			
____3.			
____4.			
____5.			
____6.			
____7.			

Be concerned but not a worrywart.

Be in awe of the process but don't stall.

E.T. was an alien, but he quickly won over those who mattered.

That is your task now.

TIPS

- Prepare, prepare, prepare.
- Know the organization.
- Know yourself.
- Develop reasons for wanting to work for a particular organization.
- In correspondence and telephone conversations invite employers to speculate, to be curious about your talents.
- Determine your uniqueness.
- Practice, practice, practice.

·   ·   ·

Preparation : Knowledge : Practice : Skill

·   ·   ·

PRINCIPLE 2.
FIRST IMPRESSIONS
COUNT, YOU BETTER
BELIEVE IT

. . .

. . .

J. Peter Grace, chairman of W. P. Grace & Company:
"The first thing you look for in a potential employee is
integrity."

Interviewer: "And how do you spot integrity?"

Mr. G: "It's a stomach reaction. I can tell whether somebody has integrity in about 40 seconds."

. . .

Forget the accuracy of Mr. Grace's stomach for a moment,
and consider the import of "40 seconds." In less than a minute
a judgment is made about one's character. Mind-boggling! Yet
Mr. Grace is not alone.

Research indicates that the *primacy effect* ("first impressions are lasting ones") is a powerful force in interviewing. Some studies show that conclusions reached in the first five minutes are decisive 85 percent of the time (see Myth #10 in Part One).

Take an example from animal research in which aversion can be induced in gerbils by injecting them with lithium chloride, causing gastrointestinal distress. One gerbil is injected shortly after being introduced to another gerbil. Forty-eight hours later the injected animal avoids the new gerbil but not others. When untreated gerbils are exposed to new acquaintances, they run up to them and in typical animal fashion sniff their body parts. Those who are injected, however, appear afraid of the stimulus animal, often moving away and hiding in a corner.

About now you're asking, What does that have to do with interviewing? Are we back to rats again?[7] Not exactly, but I think the gerbil study is a graphic way to introduce *imprinting*, that process by which events and feelings are fixed indelibly on our memories. We all can think of childhood experiences that have never left us.

In many ways the history of humankind depends on imprinting. Fossil imprints of dinosaurs, for instance, help us understand life millions of years ago. The invention of the (im)printing press made it possible to pass on wisdom from generation to generation in a permanent form.

---

[7]You recall Pavlov's dog, whose feeding was preceded by a bell. Each time the scientist rang a bell the dog salivated, anticipating dinner. You may also recall B. F. Skinner's experiments on conditioning pigeons and rats by rewarding them every time they pressed a button. Animal studies prompt such humor as the cartoon in which one rat says to another, "Watch how I've got this guy conditioned. Every time I push this button, he feeds me." Or the bulletin posted outside a psychology professor's office that asks: "Does the name Pavlov ring a bell?"

In the socialization process, clearly early impressions influence subsequent behavior. "Republican" children follow Republican traditions; lawyers breed young lawyers; Methodists tend to stay Methodist; Catholics, Catholic; college graduates rear college graduates and on and on.

Many of our current attractions or avoidances stem from forgotten experiences. In job-hunting it makes no difference whether employers can make sound judgments when first meeting you. The point is, they evaluate, and their decisions are influenced by initial impressions, many of them unconscious. Their final verdict usually coincides with those first reactions.

Therefore, attend to introductions and learn to forge a positive imprint. *Shape Up* your impressions on others. Four aspects of the *Shaping-up Process* are:

- Entrance
- Appearance
- Presence
- Openers

·   ·   ·

> You never get a second chance to make a good first impression.

·   ·   ·

Entrance

The interview begins when you walk in the door—the door of the building, not the interviewer's office. Whom you meet, how you greet them, what you say can convey a sense of confidence or indecision.

Be natural, friendly, direct, be in control. Nervous? Of course, but don't let on. Interviewing is an uncertain business for all concerned, including the interviewer. As strangers you both start on the same footing, attempting to reach a minimum comfort level.

Don't walk into the office like a question mark. Move in a straight line, maintaining eye contact. Offer a hand and introduce yourself: "I'm Eleanor Doyle, and I'm here for my two o'clock appointment with Mr. Fitzgerald."

A word about handshakes. In Western cultures we greet people by shaking hands, whether male or female. As you move through introductions at a cocktail party, you receive as many different shakes as people attending the affair. For example:

- *The Dead Fish*—For sure no blood courses through this hand, and if you squeeze too tight it will expire.
- *The Slippery Eel*—Like gripping a peeled tomato or, even worse, a hand dipped in mineral oil.
- *Say Uncle*—Usually from some beefy guy who pumps iron, leaving the impression of much brawn and no brain.
- *The Fisherman*—Where the other person jerks you back and forth, trying to reel you in.

- *The Intimate*—He or she continues to hold your hand while discussing the weather, the Cubs' chance for a pennant, and the up-and-coming mayoral election.
- *The Assembly Line*—Complete with dirty nails and usually executed from right to left.
- *The Fingertip*—This allows for a quick getaway and can be used to combat the "Say Uncle" approach.
- *The Brother*—Done palm-to-palm with all kinds of fraternal variations.
- *The High Five*—A typical jock greeting, signifying accomplishment and camaraderie.

One interviewer's view:

"Upon meeting, wait for the candidate to offer to shake hands. Did it come naturally? Was it accompanied by a pleasant smile? Or did the candidate just assume you're not a handshaker and let it slide?"

Whether or not interviewers read that much into a handshake, the responsibility for greeting is yours. Walk directly toward your inquisitors, look them in the eye, extend your hand and smile.

What kind of handshake? A natural one, dry and firm but not overpowering, and one that communicates "I'm really glad to be here."

If you feel I overstate the importance of something as simple as a handshake, test it yourself. Track how others greet you. Which ones have the most positive effect, and what do they do to create that effect? Then work out specifics of an initial greeting that fit your style.

Appearance

I can't say enough about dress. The Frankensteins of life have difficulty getting jobs and promotions.

We do judge books by their covers. Burke Market Research surveyed vice presidents and personnel directors of one hundred American corporations and discovered three out of four admitted that "good-looking" people get the promotions and make more money.

In a University of Minnesota study respondents associated a neat and attractive appearance with poise, strength, sensitivity, sincerity, intelligence and success.

Another researcher gave school superintendents résumés and photographs of prospective high school principals, with the task of rating their qualifications for the job. The résumés were identical but the photos varied in body type, from short and overweight to tall and handsome. Superintendents judged the tall lean applicants most qualified, even though résumés were the same for both groups.

Now we all can't be a Madonna or an Indiana Jones (and perhaps don't want to be), but we can shape up—physically and cosmetically. My father insisted, "Even if you're not a ballplayer, dress like one."

If the interview is an audition, a beauty contest, what can you do about it?

1. Take care of yourself—exercise and eat sensibly.
2. Treat the interview like a military inspection—spit-shine shoes, wash behind ears, cut your hair, and dress up.

What kind of clothes? That's detailed in other books.[8] The guiding principle is: Dress conservatively and dress to fit the level or position. Some writers recommend changing your suit, jewelry, glasses, watch, and even your attaché case according to the type of organization. That's overkill.

For most jobs a suit and tie, preferably brown or gray, are

[8]John T. Molloy devotes 372 pages to *Dress for Success* (New York: Warner Books, 1988).

appropriate. Women should dress modestly unless, of course, they're trying out for a Broadway chorus line.

Long before the movie we rated others "10" based on their appearances. Trial lawyers insist their clients appear in court neatly and conservatively dressed. The more heinous the charge, the more important the attire.

The same for interviewing. No matter what your lifestyle, you must appear acceptable. So leave your Grateful Dead T-shirt at home and dress somewhere between a bag lady and a maharajah. In other words, dress sensibly and with restraint.

Presence

Presence is as intangible as appearance is tangible. Presence is a demeanor, a "feel" we bring to relationships. A positive presence includes a sense of:

- Fun
- Confidence
- With-it-ness
- Naturalness

Having *fun*, enjoying life, is visible in a sense of humor, a laugh, a smile. On the next page is an advertisement for a personnel agency that claimed to go beyond the smile. Maybe the agency does, but most interviewers do not. So smile, smile, smile, and laugh when you get a chance. The interview allows no room for darkness. Let your smile hide misgivings. Try to have fun.

Confidence grows out of experience and competence. It is grounded in faith—faith in your potential, your skills and

Are you hiring
the smile?

knowledge, and in an ability to express yourself under the strain of interviewing. You're not born confident. You develop it by riding your successes and learning from failures.

With-it-ness is conveyed by being current, showing interest in the other person's activities, and knowing what's going on. Keep up with contemporary issues, and read the business section of your local newspaper. Be conversant about the company's products and services.

Naturalness can contribute to a strong positive presence, but contrary to popular notion, naturalness is not all natural. Rather than inherited, it's the result of studied practice. Performers such as Meryl Streep, Jack Nicholson, Gregory Peck, Jessica Tandy, Alec Guinness and Dustin Hoffman develop a way to become the person they are re-creating. Then they invent a technique to conceal their technology, hence giving an *au naturel* presence.

Anyone can be natural in his or her own surroundings. The trick is to do it on the interviewer's turf. The more skilled you become, the more you project ease and self-assurance. You develop a kind of superspirit—one that pervades the interview and sways the outcome, frequently without the interviewer's specific awareness.

In Malcolm Forbes's words, "Presence is more than just being there."

.   .   .

Substitute gloss for dross.

.   .   .

Openers

Finally you're in the interviewer's office. What to do now? Listen to the other side—a consultant advising "How to Conduct a Successful Sales Interview":

> Don't offer to take (and hang) the candidate's coat. Observe what is done with it. A bright, sales-minded person would have left it in your outer-office—to be prepared for action—unencumbered. When you find yourself interviewing a meek individual with a folded coat on his lap, make a mental note that your prospects and customers will be exposed to the same "dynamism."
>
> Don't go out of your way to be extra warm and friendly, to put the candidate at ease. Naturally your PR department won't agree with this. But your job is to identify candidates who can sell your product or service to prospects and customers who are not always warm and friendly. It's necessary for you to find out, even at this early stage, just how a candidate reacts to this type of treatment. After all, the biggest and most important sales are usually made to extremely busy buyers who, due to time pressures, are far from warm and friendly.

Granted, this is one person's view. I would hope your coat is not the deciding factor in whether or not you're offered a job. Also, the relationship between stress in interviews and stress in selling is questionable. Still, you must be prepared.

Whether or not interviewers follow the consultant's advice, a first meeting between strangers usually begins with inertia. Most of the time you must *jump-start* the interviewer.

How do you jump-start?

- Talk about an interviewer interest, e.g., a painting in the office, something in the waiting room, pictures of the interviewer's children, an item you read about the organization.

- Start with something to laugh about, e.g., a happening on the way to the interview, a human interest story in the news. Stay away from jokes. Unless you tell a relevant one, you may find yourself spraying ether.

- Invite the interviewer to speculate, e.g., "I see from the photos on the wall that you've been to St. Martin. I was there three years ago." Stop. It's almost impossible for the interviewer not to inquire further: "Do you know Mullet Bay?" or "Did you scuba dive there?" The rumor mill in organizations is a prime example of an "invitation to speculate." Where partial information is provided, our minds seek to complete the sentence and fill in the blanks.

- Violate the interviewer's expectations. An example is a magician who surprises us and, therefore, has our rapt attention. One tack is to ask the first question—about the secretary, the interviewer, the building. Or you might start by unfolding some of your homework: "Yesterday I visited a store that sells your products, and learned some interesting things talking to the assistant manager."

Jump-starting begins with concerns of interviewers. Involve them—get them to laugh, smile, ask questions, to show enthusiasm. A sample scenario might go like this:

The secretary announces Mr. Durney. He walks directly toward the interviewer, extends his hand, smiles and says, "Hi, I'm Tod Durney."

"I'm Anthony Wheaton. Good to meet you. Please sit down."

As they're settling in, Durney scans the room. "I notice your trophy on the shelf. Are you a tennis player?"

"Yes, of sorts. That's a club trophy."

"Oh, where do you play?"

"At the Saw Mill Club in Riverton. Every year they have singles and doubles tournaments. My partner and I have won the doubles two years in a row."

"Wow, sounds like you're a serious player. I've been watching the U.S. Open on TV. Saw the Jimmy Connors–Krickstein match. Unbelievable."

"Yes, wasn't that something. Thirty-nine years old and Connors beats him in a fifth set tie-breaker. You know, I'm younger than Connors, and I'm worn out after three sets."

"I know what you mean. I played a few sets over Labor Day weekend, and I'm still stiff."

"Oh, you play?"

"Once every couple weeks."

"Well, it's a great conditioner. Play more often. I think everyone should be taught tennis in school. It's one sport you can play all your life. At the club we have a number of eighty-year-olds who are out there every day."

"That's great. I bet when they use the word *stroke,* it doesn't refer to a forehand or backhand."

[*Laughter*]

"I'm glad you enjoy tennis, Tod. What else do you do in your leisure time?"

"Well, I like . . ."

Tod is off to a roaring start. There's much more ahead, but an excellent beginning nonetheless.

.   .   .

> Opening is finding your skater's edge. Once you've accomplished that, you're ready to demonstrate figure eights.

.   .   .

You better believe first impressions make a difference. You must orchestrate love at first sight. Above all, ensure that the initial look does not trigger dislike—or worse, indifference.

Time may sanctify, but you don't have time. The interview is a Christmas card event, a stop-sign happening. Get out of your starting blocks fast. The employment office is no place for pusillanimity. The meek may inherit the earth, but they'll go unemployed.

Enter with style—something less than fanfare, but don't be afraid to toot your horn. Score the tune, and measure by measure play it on soft pedal with assurance, with care, and with pride.

TIPS

- Shape up (even chess players do that).
- Freshen up—don't be a barn breath.
- Show up on time.
- Dress with propriety—in style but not dashing.
- Project friendliness in the first minute.
- Convey confidence with eye contact and a firm handshake.
- Smile—it goes a long way to establish rapport.
- Bridge the gap with conversation of interest to the interviewer.

PRINCIPLE 3. CROSS THE ROAD TO REACH THE MIDDLE

• • •

Before reading this chapter, rate yourself on the items below. They can provide a general indication of your leanings. Circle the number on each scale that represents you. Be honest in your responses; there are no right or wrong answers. For best results don't think too long on any one item. Record your first impulse by circling the number on each scale that best describes you. For example, the first item: If you are very friendly, score a 5 or 6; if slightly aloof, circle 3.

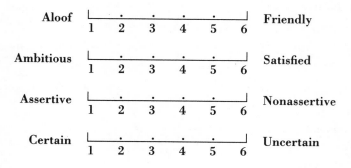

Aloof	1 2 3 4 5 6	Friendly
Ambitious	1 2 3 4 5 6	Satisfied
Assertive	1 2 3 4 5 6	Nonassertive
Certain	1 2 3 4 5 6	Uncertain

Confident	. . . .	1 2 3 4 5 6	Insecure

Confident   1 2 3 4 5 6   Insecure

Conservative   1 2 3 4 5 6   Liberal

Deliberate   1 2 3 4 5 6   Impulsive

Dependent   1 2 3 4 5 6   Independent

Down-to-Earth   1 2 3 4 5 6   Scholarly

Efficient   1 2 3 4 5 6   Inefficient

Exacting   1 2 3 4 5 6   "Loose"

A Feeler   1 2 3 4 5 6   A Thinker

Prefer Fiction   1 2 3 4 5 6   Prefer Nonfiction

Happy-Go-Lucky   1 2 3 4 5 6   Serious

Individualistic   1 2 3 4 5 6   Conformist

A Few Interests   1 2 3 4 5 6   Many Interests

Introvert   1 2 3 4 5 6   Extrovert

Lackadaisical   1 2 3 4 5 6   Energetic

Leader							Follower
	.	.	.	.			
	1	2	3	4	5	6	

Listener							Talker
	.	.	.	.			
	1	2	3	4	5	6	

Leader · · · · Follower
1 2 3 4 5 6

Listener · · · · Talker
1 2 3 4 5 6

Neat · · · · Sloppy
1 2 3 4 5 6

Optimistic · · · · Pessimistic
1 2 3 4 5 6

Organized · · · · Disorganized
1 2 3 4 5 6

Other-Centered · · · · Self-Centered
1 2 3 4 5 6

People-Oriented · · · · Task-Oriented
1 2 3 4 5 6

A Planner · · · · A Doer
1 2 3 4 5 6

Practical · · · · Idealistic
1 2 3 4 5 6

A Praiser · · · · A Critic
1 2 3 4 5 6

Quiet · · · · Outspoken
1 2 3 4 5 6

Realistic · · · · Romantic
1 2 3 4 5 6

Relaxed · · · · Tense
1 2 3 4 5 6

Reserved · · · · Outgoing
1 2 3 4 5 6

	1	2	3	4	5	6	
Risk-Taker							Cautious
Straightforward							"Roundabout"
Traditional							Innovative
Subordinate							Dominant
Concerned with Things							Concerned with Ideas
Timid							Venturesome
Trusting							Suspicious
Uncontrolled							Controlled
Work-Oriented							Play-Oriented

Now you have a profile of sorts for your interests, strengths and inclinations. We will come back to it later in the chapter.

The title of this chapter is an *answer*: Cross the road to reach the middle. The *question*: What should interviewees do when they come to the crossroads?

Humans yearn to lose themselves in a crowd, not to be singled out unless for accomplishment and accolade. Early on, children learn to play it safe. If there's one chance in a thousand to look stupid in school, they hide behind each other and stare at the floor.

How many times have you sat in a meeting where only a

few participate? Could the others contribute? Of course, but the fear of being wrong or out of step prevents them from doing so. How many times have you observed group members saying something "far out" and concluded they were radical, unstable or at best a little weird? We have tissue-paper tolerance for deviance.

Interviewers are turned off by excess. The guiding principle of this chapter is: *Avoid extremes.*

A dramatic case demonstrates this. In 1988 the Senate Judiciary Committee interviewed Robert H. Bork, President Bush's nominee for United States Supreme Court justice. Bork, who had an impressive legal background, took forceful positions on many issues. The Senate rejected him.

In 1991 Judge Clarence Thomas, another Bush nominee (with a less impressive legal history), repeatedly avoided controversial issues, especially abortion, by talking around them or claiming no comment or no opinion. On one occasion the Senate panel's chairman, Joseph R. Biden, Jr., retorted, "That's the most unartful dodge I ever heard." Thomas was confirmed.

"PC" is a label popular on college campuses. It stands for "Politically Correct," and refers to persons who say the right things and take the right actions approved by the group of which they are a part. During the interview wear your "PC" pin.

Forget revolution and reform. Play it close to the vest. Physically, mentally and emotionally tightrope the median.

On page 89 are characteristics associated with "middle of the road" thinking. A pie-in-the-sky list, of course. Obviously no one lives up to this profile, yet interviewers continue to search for Prince Valiant and Princess Leia. As noted in Part One, most of these traits cannot be observed in an interview, which means managers infer them from scant information.

Go back to the beginning of the chapter and compare your profile with the "middle of the road" list. Check every scale you rated 1–2 or 5–6. You may want to consider toning down these traits. For instance, if you appear too relaxed, too timid, too humble, too sensitive, too cautious, interviewers might conclude you're wishy-washy. Or *extremely outgoing, dominant, tough-minded, assertive* may mean "unmanageable." (Even *all work and no play* could translate into "Nay.")

One pressing question emerges: How can you create the perception of some of these Scout qualities in interviews? Here are suggestions and sample scripts to trigger your thinking.

The Work Ethic—"In my family, as kids we shouldered responsibility for the chores. I worked my way through college. I don't think in terms of week and weekend. For me there are seven days, and all are workdays when I have a project to complete."

Rags to Riches—We still put a halo over the Horatio Algers of the world. If you come from modest beginnings, it helps; even better if your family immigrated from the "Old Country." Elaborate on what it took to get you where you are. If you happen to be "North Shore," don't flaunt it. Let it stand for "well bred."

Dependability—"I'm a bear when it comes to finishing a task on time. In three years on the college newspaper I never missed a deadline. Of course, that included some all-night sessions, some hair-pulling and foot stomping, but that goes with the territory, I guess. The editor knew I would always be there when needed."

Middle of the Road

What is "middle"? Some and all of the following:

a work ethic
a rags-to-riches past
promotability
a business bent
enthusiasm
verbal facility
patriotism
sincerity
honesty
sociability
decisiveness
down-to-earth quality
flexibility
commitment
poise under pressure
humility
cooperativeness
courage
financial stability
tough-mindedness
a finisher
orderliness
ability to inspire others
ability to see the broad
    picture

competence
dependability
a jock background
that Jack Armstrong look
maturity
team player
alertness
an astronaut image
initiative
courtesy
intelligence
confidence
self-motivation
problem solver
loyalty
warmth
leadership
willingness to accept
    criticism
a "good company person"
sense of responsibility
self-discipline
conscientiousness
creativity
stability

A Jock—Best if you participated in interscholastic athletics. Stay away from intramurals, they're rinky-dink. In lieu of competitive sports, explain: "I work out every day. Bought one of those stationary bikes for the winter. Also I've been taking skiing lessons. My instructor says I'm at the intermediate level. If I don't break a leg, my aim is to be an advanced skier by next season."

That Jack Armstrong Look—Obviously you eat the "breakfast of champions" and follow neat grooming habits.[9]

A business bent—"I plan. I think through tasks. I take them step by step. I match my approach to the situation."

Maturity—Ann Landers defines *maturity* as "the ability to do a job whether or not you are supervised, to carry money without spending it, and to bear an injustice without wanting to get even." Employers are enamored of the word *mature*. "We want mature people," they say, which usually means employees who "will not panic under pressure or do anything to embarrass us." So conduct yourself accordingly during the interview.

Enthusiasm—"High energy level" is a buzz phrase in the employment field. An enthusiastic approach in the interview will be interpreted as High Energy Level—a person HEL-bent on getting the job done. Principle 7 expands on ways to create a spirited interview.

---

[9]Adding to our discussion of dress and demeanor in Principle 2, a University of Nebraska study showed that long hair evoked an intense negative reaction in interviewers over forty years of age.

Team Player—"I love symphonic music. A few years ago I went to a performance conducted by Leonard Bernstein. He ended with Tchaikovsky's *1812 Overture* complete with full orchestra, chorus and cannons. It was awesome. Afterward, I began to reflect on how each musician can produce beautiful solo music, but together they surpassed what any individual could do. For a few hours I witnessed human beings at their noblest. This is the power of team play, I think—the capacity to go far beyond the accomplishment of any one member.

"At the end before Bernstein took a bow, he insisted the chorus and orchestra stand and receive the first ovation. That's the essence of teamwork—members giving credit where credit is due with no one individual hogging the limelight."

Verbal Facility—Probably no single skill has greater influence on the outcome of interviews than the ability to express yourself clearly and interestingly. I devote a whole chapter to it in Principle 6.

Alertness—This can best be demonstrated by:

- Responding quickly
- Noticing things around you
- Picking up on specific thoughts or words of interviewers
- Practicing active listening (see page 161)

Patriotism—The 1991 Gulf War evoked a swell of patriotism not seen in the United States since World War II. Amid this atmosphere a comedian sang a grating rendition of "The Star-Spangled Banner," a rock star refused to begin her concert with the national anthem, and a basketball player chose not to wear an American flag on his jersey. All were ostracized.

Whatever your dove/hawk persuasions, choose the time and place to express them. The interview is not that time and place. Instead, focus on things you like about the country. If it fits the conversation throw in the virtues of self-government, voting, activeness in community affairs such as Rotary Club, church, the PTA.

The Astronaut—If you saw the movie *The Right Stuff*, you know what to look and be like.

Stability—It helps if you have progressed normally—high school, college (if required), then at least three years on a job before transferring. Don't be a globe-trotter. The interviewer must be convinced of two things:

1. You can hold a job and will commit to the organization.
2. Once in the position you will behave in predictable and harmonious ways.

•   •   •

> In job-hopping, leapers become lepers.

•   •   •

Sincerity—The look on the face of someone with hemorrhoids. Of course it's more: an absence of deceit and pretense, usually demonstrated by a genuine interest in and concern for others. Famous examples of sincerity include Mother Teresa, Jimmy Stewart, Anwar Sadat, Bill Moyers, Abraham Lincoln, Walter Cronkite, Albert Schweitzer, Robert Fulghum and Bambi.

Initiative—"It seems I'm always starting something. As a kid I would be the first to set up a lemonade stand in our block. In school I formed a group that would go out to Sunnyrest and entertain senior citizens. I organized college squads to conduct Saturday morning environmental cleanup campaigns. I get a kick out of looking for things to do rather than waiting for someone to give me instructions."

Honesty—It should be clear from Principle 4 that I don't believe honesty is necessarily the best policy when you're looking for a job. Nor is honesty discernible in the interview. But as long as interviewers think they can judge truthfulness, you must create a credible image. The next chapter discusses this question at length.

Courtesy—Avoid bluntness and being too straightforward. Make ample use of civilized lubricants:

- "In my opinion . . ."
- "It appears to me that . . ."
- "That's a good point."
- "You may be right; however, another way to look at it . . ."
- "I appreciate your saying that."
- "I'm not sure I agree, but I see your side of it."
- "Thanks for your time."

Also avoid talking disparagingly about former employers. It makes *you* look bad rather than them.

Sociability—Here's what interviewers look for:

- Have you had problems with teachers or supervisors?
- Are you able to deal calmly and patiently with short-comings of colleagues?
- Do you get along with others?
- Are you well liked?
- Were you in a fraternity or sorority or part of some group that indicates you're not a hermit?

Decisiveness—A comic routine used to go something like this: "I'm in charge. I know what I'm doing." (All said in a macho manner.) "Why, I make decisions just like that!" ("That" being the snap of two fingers, but the comic can't get his to snap until after four or five tries.)

Interviewers want to feel that given a set of alternatives, you will be able to "snap to" and take action.

One kind of scenario: "I wrote to thirteen colleges with good reputations in the liberal arts. Seven sent form replies and I discarded them. I talked to alumni of the other six and visited the campuses. Finally I chose Lawrence University because it was solid academically, and they had a more personal approach to education. I wouldn't be a number there, and would have many opportunities to interact with faculty and other students."

Decisiveness is a key theme in Principle 7.

A down-to-earth quality—"Jobs at all levels have a sweat and gutter component. I expect that. My grandparents worked in the factory and on construction. They taught me the value of getting my hands dirty. Even after college when I came home, I was expected to do chores like everyone else."

Let interviewers know that you accept dog duty (versus fat cat work) as part of any employment.

Intelligence—Short of administering an IQ test,[10] interviewers cannot possibly judge your intelligence, even though they claim to. Present one novel idea and they will think you possess superior intellect. Principle 6 and Principle 7 speak on this matter.

Confidence—"I have had more successes than failures so far in my career. I remember once coming home from football practice dejected. My father asked, 'What's wrong?' I told him I had tried to block the defensive end on a new play and missed every time. The coach never stopped yelling at me. My father said calmly, 'Well, why are you so upset? What'd you learn?'

"What did he mean, what did I learn? I was so embarrassed I wanted to hide.

"Now I understand. Failures are stepping-stones to success. They tell me what I'm missing, what I don't know, and what I need to achieve. That experience has stuck with me and helped me attempt new tasks with confidence."

In addition to *confidence* scenarios, ask questions that indicate you're not afraid. And, of course, your poise and presence can give an aura of assurance.

Self-motivation—Show rather than tell. Relate projects or talents that you have developed on your own, e.g., photography, teaching yourself to play an instrument, enrolling in night courses, or starting a club, a new department, a business.

Example: "I consider myself a self-starter. In school I

[10]Even an IQ test does not measure intelligence. It measures how well one does on an IQ test, and is heavily weighted toward memory of numbers and words.

taught myself to play the guitar and did some dance gigs on weekends. Last year before I went to France for the summer, I took a Berlitz course and was able to converse understandably with the natives. At MPI I ran a safety campaign on my own; it wasn't an assigned part of my job. Our department ended the year with the best safety record."

Flexibility—"I welcome new assignments. The greater the variety on the job, the better I like it. In my current position I manage many responsibilities simultaneously—acting as a liaison with the sales force, handling complaints, conducting customer surveys, planning preliminary budgets, and that elusive elastic clause: doing whatever else my boss assigns.

"Also you can see by my application that MPI has relocated me three times in the last five years. That's okay with me—gives me a chance to see what life is like in different parts of the country."

Avoid irrefutable statements. Don't dig a hole you can't fill. Never take unyielding stands on any issue.

.   .   .

> Walk the line rather than draw it. The interview's not the Alamo.

.   .   .

Problem-solving—Cite a work-related problem where you:

- Defined it
- Identified causes
- Invented alternative solutions
- Selected the best one based on desirability, probability, practicality and the risks involved

- Tested it
- Adapted and implemented the solution as dictated by test results

That's the classic problem-solving model and will do for interviews. When asked about a work situation one applicant gave this example:

"Artie was a maintenance man on the same shift that Linda tended the toolcrib. Every time Artie requested a new bit for a drill press, they got into an argument. The problem escalated until production was being affected because Artie wasn't keeping equipment maintained.

"I observed them in action and interviewed each separately. As far as I could tell, there were a number of possible causes: Artie didn't like working with women; Linda was untrained; they had incompatible personalities; the system for checking out tools was faulty; the system wasn't being followed; other shifts were misplacing parts; poor communication; lack of teamwork.

"I considered a number of solutions: Tell Artie and Linda to shape up or get out; call a general meeting of the whole shop to discuss the toolcrib process; change the system; train Linda or transfer her; talk to the other shifts; let Artie and Linda work it out for themselves.

"After weighing the alternatives, I assigned Artie to the toolcrib for one hour a day to help train Linda. After a week the three of us met and assessed the situation. Miraculously it worked. They were nicer to each other, Artie was repairing equipment on time, and we were keeping to our production schedules."

Commitment—If you had to choose between completing a report and a dinner engagement (or a ball game or playing golf), you would stay on the job. And when you make a career choice, you stick with it.

Poise under pressure—It would help if you had rescued a helpless child from a raging inferno, but barring that, note stress situations you have managed. How about handling an irate customer or meeting a last-minute schedule change?

Example: "A customer came in upset that the 'tap-tap' in her car was not fixed. Now anyone knows that random noises in the body of an auto are near impossible to diagnose. First I took her into the office, gave her a cup of coffee, let her vent her emotions and indicated I knew how annoying this could be. Then we drove the car together. As you might guess, no rattle. So I gave her my card and told her to call me, day or night, the next time it happened. She thanked me and left in a better frame of mind.

"I don't know if we'll ever find the source of the 'tap-tap,' but at least I want her to understand we care."

Warmth—Refer back to the discussion of *presence* in Principle 2. Warmth emanates from a smile, a handshake and your ease during interviews.

Leadership—One of the most revered qualities in our culture. Make sure you have been elected or appointed in charge of things, e.g., extracurricular activities, a committee, athletic team, task force or community project. Suggest how people look to you for direction at the office. *Leading* is the theme in Principle 7.

Humility—Recognize others' contributions to your success. Make a list of influencial people in your life and be prepared to talk about their contributions. A major leaguer[11] who had just pitched a no-hitter was quoted: "I'm overwhelmed. I don't know what to say. Above all, my teammates deserve the credit. They were fantastic on defense. Without them it never would have been possible."

Be humble but not deer-shy.

Loyalty—"I have a high LQ. That's my acronym for Loyalty Quotient. Ask my colleagues and they'll tell you I stand by those I believe in. Our industry, for instance, has been receiving criticism of late. I speak at community functions—Rotary, chamber of commerce, Lions, church groups—giving our side of the controversy. I mean, why join an organization if you're not going to back it?"

A Good Company Person—See *Loyalty*.

Financial Stability—Any of the following will do:

- "I started earning money with a four-thirty-in-the-morning paper route and have supported myself ever since."
- "I'm proud to say I worked my way through college."
- "Currently I'm treasurer at the church, and I don't mind taking some of the credit for moving from the red to the black in three years."

---

[11]That was Len Barker of the Cleveland Indians. Actually, he pitched a perfect nine-inning game—twenty-seven batters, twenty-seven outs. Nobody reached base. After the game he called his elderly grandmother to tell her the good news. She replied, "That's good, and I hope you do better next time."

- "When I took over my territory at MPI, sales were down by a third. Now volume has more than doubled, and next year I expect to be even better."
- "I keep a monthly personal budget, because I discovered long ago that without it, expenses will always exceed revenues."

Willingness to Accept Criticism—Don't have "rabbit ears," my father's term for a baseball player whose performance was diminished by the taunts and criticisms of the opposing team. Example: "My first year of teaching, I was having a terrible time. I ended every week with a throbbing headache. One day one of my colleagues said, 'Hey, you're too hard on the students, loosen up.'

"I was upset at first, then I realized she was right. I had blinders on. I was uptight. I wasn't having any fun.

"Now my approach is to meet periodically with colleagues and ask them to critique my work. It helps me get perspective on what I'm doing."

Tough-mindedness—Point out a case where you made an unpopular decision (cutting the budget, disciplining or firing an employee, standing up for a colleague) that turned out in the best interest of those involved. You set high standards for yourself and those around you.

Self-discipline—"If I've learned anything, it's this: The demands of the job always seem to exceed the time needed to meet them. And procrastination runs rampant. I try to cope with this in three ways:

1. Each morning I jot down on a three-by-five card one or two things to accomplish before the end of the day, then start with those.

2.   On Sunday night I take fifteen minutes to write out what I want to achieve during the week.

3.   Deadlines, I set deadlines for important tasks. Without them I find things just don't get done."

Creativity—Ben Franklin wrote, "To cease to think creatively is but little different from ceasing to live." Even though organizations reward conformity, more and more they are recognizing big Ben's meaning. Their survival depends on invention.

Many corporations provide training in creativity, emphasizing right-brain, left-brain thinking. As the theory goes, people lean one way or the other. If left brain you tend to be logical, technical, rational. If right brain you are more intuitive, emotional, artistic.

Though the theme of this chapter is moderation, interviewers do look for signs of creativity (not kookiness, please). For ways to appear creative see Principle 6 and Principle 7.

Competence—Demonstrate all of the above but not in excess.

Organizations polish employees like mirrors until they reflect each other. Interviewers seek facsimiles of themselves (Myth #7 in Part One).

Don't make waves.[12] The corporate world isn't looking for more runaways.

·   ·   ·

> Polar behavior may be more exciting but will chill your chances.

·   ·   ·

A sixteen-foot crocodile can swallow up to ten pounds of stone, or about one percent of its body weight, which acts as ballast so it can remain submerged except for its snout and eyes, watching for prey. The ballast is held forward enough to counter the heavy weight of the tail. You need that even-keeled look, so mainline a few middle-class values.

To pass muster swallow a bedrock of hard work, stick-to-itiveness, ambition and well-roundedness. On the forty-one scales at the beginning of this chapter, lean toward the center.

[12]Maybe a ripple or two. See Principle 7.

TIPS

- Avoid cleavage of any kind.
- The preppy/yuppie look is still in vogue.
- Be ambitious, assertive, confident—but not too.
- Don't reveal offbeat hobbies and activities.
- Don't admit to being an opera or a heavy-metal buff.
- Demonstrate initiative and organization by your readiness for the interview.
- Don't walk the plank on any issue.
- "Neither a borrower nor a lender be."
- "Courtesy" is the interviewee's watchword.
- Balance:

  talking with listening

  giving with seeking information

  formality with informality

  personal with professional.
- When in doubt, list to starboard.

Principle 4.
Honesty Is Not the
Best Policy

• • •

The world would be as unmanageable with absolute truth as with unrestrained falsehood.

Honesty is not the best policy—necessarily. This chapter begins with a short treatise on Truth and Morality and ends with an application, Honesty in the Interview.

Truth and Morality

Try to explain two sentences: the one below and the one on the next page.

THE SENTENCE ON THE TOP OF THE NEXT PAGE IS FALSE.

THE SENTENCE ON THE BOTTOM OF THE PREVIOUS PAGE IS TRUE.

Making sense of these two statements is like a cat trying to catch its tail. The sentences are a notorious liar's paradox. You cannot tell truth because they contradict each other, as do many life situations.

Often uncovering a lie is as difficult as uncovering truth. To identify lies experts look for such verbal clues as being evasive, answering questions hesitatingly or too slowly, talking too much and contradicting oneself. More important are non-verbal tip-offs like fidgeting, looking away, clearing the throat, a strained or weak-sounding voice, a fake smile. Still, researchers have found that these experts—judges, police, psychiatrists, agents of the FBI and CIA, even polygraph operators—perform no better at detecting lies than if they had guessed randomly.

Even if interviewers were accurate lie detectors, the thesis of this chapter would be the same. My aim is to place dishonesty in perspective. I realize some critics may label my view "immoral," but to paraphrase Ring Lardner, so are all writings based on truth.

Honesty is part of the fabric of our society. It is underscored in the Boy Scout oath, the West Point Academy honor code ("A member of the brigade does not lie, cheat or steal"), school textbooks (e.g., George Washington's confession that he cut down his father's cherry tree and Honest Abe Lincoln) and in our jurisprudence system ("to tell the truth so help you God").[13]

---

[13]Even under oath the whole truth is seldom told. A favorite response in the Watergate and Iran-Contra hearings was, "I don't remember." Prosecutors and defense attorneys present only that portion of truth that makes their cases appear just and right.

In that moral climate advocating dishonesty is like selling a guillotine to cure migraines. Yet we all lie. One psychological study estimated that each of us tells an average of two lies per day. Hamlet went further: "To be honest, as this world goes, is to be one man pick'd out of ten thousand."

.   .   .

Some Day-to-Day Dishonesties

Advertisement: "Guaranteed waterproof."
Overweight Person: "I'm going on a diet tomorrow."
Dentist: "This won't take much longer."
Realtor: "I'll get you top dollar for your house."
Son: "I'll be right there, Mom."
Mom: "This'll hurt me more than it'll hurt you."
Gambler: "I broke about even."
Clerk: "It's on order."
Military Spokesman: "We are moving our tanks across your border to promote the peace."
Husband: "I had to work late at the office."
Car Salesman: "It was only driven to and from church by a little old lady."
Politician: "Read my lips—no new taxes."

.   .   .

Despite moral vows, why dishonesty? Three reasons come to mind:

1.   A normal gap exists between thinking and doing, between what we intend and what we are able to deliver. We are plagued with the desire to live perfect lives but lack the equipment to pull it off. Still, it is our shortcomings (e.g., our lies) that set us apart. Beauty in nature can be found in imperfection.

2. We judge our actions on *honest intent*, while others may perceive only *dishonest results*. Truth is always in the eye of the beholder. What management states as fact union representatives see as lies, and vice versa. In the ongoing Arab–Israeli conflict all parties are convinced their position is the true one.

Remember the story of the blind men asked to describe an elephant. The one near the trunk said, "It's a thick hose." The man in the rear replied, "No, it's a rope." Another, next to one of the elephant's legs, concluded, "It's a log." A fourth, standing broadside, contradicted: "You're all crazy—an elephant is something without a beginning or end." And so on.

We view the world from where we stand. In the 1988 Gary Hart affair *The Miami Herald* maintained that its stakeout of his home was in the name of good journalism. Hart claimed it was a violation of privacy that triggered a series of innuendoes and vicious lies.

3. Certain circumstances dictate untruth as the prudent course of action. On occasion we lie to save ourselves or others from hurt.

"I'D LIKE TO SAY THIS IS A DELICIOUS MEAL, BUT I WAS BROUGHT UP TO TELL THE TRUTH."

"HAVE I EVER LIED TO YOU UNLESS I HAD TO?"

In the Iran-Contra hearings Colonel Oliver North stated, "It's better to tell lies than lose lives." Basic philosophy courses pose questions like:

- If a murderer asks where your friend is, do you lie?
- If a law enforcement officer asks the same question in order to hang your friend for a crime he didn't commit, do you lie?
- If your mother is critically ill and asks about your brother who has just died in an automobile crash, do you tell, knowing the shock may kill her?

The fact is, in the nitty-gritty carryings-on of living, we sometimes falsify unintentionally out of ignorance or misperception.

Or we may deliberately white-lie to:

- Guard our privacy
- Prevent others from taking unfair advantage
- Gain acceptance (e.g., get elected)
- Keep a confidentiality
- Protect the feelings of others
- Make a point
- Avoid an argument over the delectability of fried liver
- Excuse ourselves from one of those boring slide presentations of a trip to the Badlands
- Be modest

In a press conference Ed Koch, then mayor of New York City, argued that "white lies are okay when letting an inadequate employee go or when someone's dying of cancer."

When E. N. Adams was asked why S: *Portrait of a Spy* is a novel, he replied, "I decided that I could tell more of the truth in a fictional context." Picasso described painting as "a lie that tells the truth." For instance, to depict a cube you must draw a series of unsquares. Sir Laurence Olivier defined acting as "convincing lying." In one sense most art forms exaggerate to convey reality.

The moral, religious and social issues around honesty and dishonesty cannot be resolved here. This is not a book on norms, on what *ought* to be. I attempt to describe *what is* the current state of interviewing and how it affects you.

Perhaps the best way to end this section is with two points of view—Grandmother's and Aldous Huxley's. My Norwegian grandmother invented one of the great lie detectors of all time. She warned, "If you lie, you'll get freckles on your nose."

Huxley concluded, "You shall know the truth and the truth shall make you mad."

REPRINTED WITH SPECIAL PERMISSION OF KING FEATURES SYNDICATE

Honesty in the Interview

"The truth, the whole truth, and nothing but the truth" is not and never has been a formula for getting a job. Failure to recognize this will place you among the unemployed.

If honesty is absolute it should go both ways. Yes, interviewers lie, or at least shade the truth. Some sample dishonesties include:

- "You can be completely open with me."
- "To be perfectly honest with you . . ."
- "We'll keep your résumé on file."
- "I want you to know I'm genuinely interested in you."
- "We believe in people first and profit second."
- "Let me tip my hand. . . ."
- "We're an equal opportunity employer."
- "I know this job is below your minimum salary expectation, but we'll review and adjust it in six months."
- "You're overqualified."
- "You'll hear from us."
- "There's opportunity for rapid advancement here."
- "We want inventive, creative people in our organization."
- "Salary is no problem, if you meet the qualifications."
- "We follow an open-door policy."
- "We're not looking for yes-men; we want people who speak what's on their mind."
- "There are plenty of opportunities here for women in management."

- "This has been an interesting interview."
- "Don't answer this if you feel it's too personal."
- "I don't mean to pry."

The *Before* interview at the beginning of the book ends with an often repeated lie: "Don't call us, we'll call you." When interviewers advise something to that effect, it's a brush-off. You'll never hear from them again.

"Twenty-five years ago an employer told him, 'Don't call us, we'll call you!'"

From your experiences you can probably add other samples of interviewing foolery. Hedging abounds on both sides.

Does this mean I advocate "unrestrained falsehood"? Of course not. Here are some defined limits, some principles to guide your actions.

Honesty-Is-Not-the-Best-Policy Guidelines

1. *The relationship must be able to bear the weight of the honesty.*

    Your relationship with interviewers is fragile at best and should be handled with care. It cannot tolerate too great a deviance from the expected, so keep to yourself such information as:

    - You look at this job as a stepping-stone to bigger and richer opportunities with other organizations
    - Reasons for leaving your last position other than to better yourself
    - Personal idiosyncrasies and quirks
    - Negative family history (drinking, criminal record)
    - You're going through a messy divorce
    - Unusual lifestyle

2. *Keep it simple.*

Don't get involved in complicated fabrications. Build on your life experience so you don't have to keep track of competing stories.

3. *Stay true to the basics.*

State education and experience accurately. Don't tout a college you haven't attended, a degree you don't hold, or a company for which you have not worked. Needless to say, use your correct name and address.

Samuel Butler expressed the thought when he quipped, "I do not mind lying, but I hate inaccuracy."

4. *Don't puff.*

Remember Icarus, who, in escaping from Crete, gets carried away and flies so high that the sun melts the wax used to fasten his wings, and he falls to his death in the sea. Don't go overboard in praise of yourself. Puffery is out, e.g.:

- "The department couldn't get along without me."
- "I was the best player on the team."
- Overuse of "I"-this and "I"-that.

Overstatement is in, e.g.:

- "I believe I made a major contribution to the department by installing a new compensation and incentive system."
- "It was a championship team, and I was fortunate to be captain and one of the leading scorers."

- "We" exceeded sales quotas, "we" reduced turnover by 50 percent.

5. *Don't be somebody you're not.*

The Great Imposter may have had a life of variety and excitement, but he ended up in jail. Don't try to impersonate an engineer, a lawyer, an accomplished musician, someone fluent in Russian, a research chemist or the like.

Stick to your guns.

On the next page is a job description for a Marketing Assistant in the Consumer Products Division of Metropolitan Products Inc. (MPI). MPI is a fictitious Fortune 500 conglomerate. Assume you are applying for the job. How would you organize information about yourself to accommodate the position?

As we work through this example, consider four ways to "stretch the truth" in interviewing:

- Embellish
- Slant
- Edit
- Highlight

. . .

MPI Job Description for Marketing Assistant

1. Handle all phases of administration, including:
   - Compiling statistical data
   - Rendering reports
   - Communicating with staff and salespeople
   - Checking customer complaints
   - Assisting in marketing research
2. Answer telephone inquiries from sales representatives and customers.
3. Assist and render direction and guidance to the sales force on administrative matters.
4. Keep in continuous contact with product mangers.
5. Review company policies and ensure that marketing and sales personnel are up-to-date on them.
6. Act as liaison to other departments.
7. Screen and prepare budgets for outside services— e.g., artwork, scripts, and promotion pieces.
8. In addition the Marketing Assistant should have potential for promotion and becoming actively involved in such activities as advertising, forecasting, seeking out new ideas, supervising, planning, and organizing.

. . .

Embellish

By *embellish* I mean spruce up, add to, make more beautiful. The Marketing Assistant looks like a little-bit-of-everything job, so add some grace notes to that effect:

- You type letters for more than one person: "In my current position I have to keep track of six people's schedules, plus coordinate their activities."
- You estimate cost of supplies: "I assist in the preparation of budgets for my department."
- You type reports: "I help put together reports on product activity in different markets."
- You answer the phone for two managers: "I handle requests and complaints from salespeople and customers."

Touch up your experience to fit the job by adding detail and expanding responsibilities. Think of it as decorating a Christmas tree, improving the original with ornaments to attract attention and enhance beauty.

Slant

Slanting involves appealing to a particular interest. One thread running through the Marketing Assistant's job is coordinating and communicating with staff, sales reps, product managers, personnel from other departments and outside vendors. Direct the discussion to center on your experience and activities in this area.

Example: "Much of the time in my current position is spent interacting with the various departments. I coordinate production schedules with the plant and administrative details with sales. Product managers come to me when they want to conduct surveys in the regions. I spend an average of two hours a day on the telephone to these people. Plus it's my responsibility to keep everyone updated on policies and procedures."

Like an impressionistic painting, or better yet, taking a picture, you focus on one area to the exclusion of others.

Edit

Editing is the process of adding, deleting, and arranging your experience to fit the job. In this case you should jot down to the right of the eight responsibilities your qualifications that indicate you can perform those tasks. Edit out any experiences that may imply lack of fitness.

In an interview for the position of international product manager, one applicant mentioned his hobby: "I raise plants in my closet." *Bong*—red flag—reject. Dismissed because he was "weird." Had the interviewer probed he would have discovered that this multilingual candidate (six languages) was an amateur botanist who experimented with hybrid plants in a closet because it was the only controlled lighting and heating space available in his small apartment.

The applicant should have kept that particular avocation to himself. When in doubt about something in your background, leave it on the editing floor.

Highlight

Get out your Magic Marker and highlight qualities that suit the organization. Spotlight the most important, the most interesting aspects of your life relevant to the job description.

A woman applying for Marketing Assistant (yes, the job is real but not in MPI) mentioned that she had no history in developing budgets but added, "I'm a quick learner and I don't have math anxiety." Despite that bit of honesty, she was rejected for not being "statistically oriented."

If you're going to give prominence to pieces of yourself, make sure it's in your best interest. She should have highlighted: "I've always been fascinated with figures and statistics. My father was an accountant and insisted that my sisters and I take a full measure of mathematics in school. In each of my previous jobs I've always participated in budget planning."

.   .   .

A lie in time saves nine (rejects).

.   .   .

A Word on Tests

Avoid taking them, not because they're bad but because they are badly interpreted. Test results tend to dominate all other information about you. Refuse to take a lie-detector test. In 1988 Congress banned random polygraph examinations and most uses of the device for pre-employment purposes.[14]

If you must test, do the following:

First, understand the job and key qualities the employer is looking for.

Leadership?   Someone who will make changes and inspire others.

---

[14]Not covered by the law are federal, state and local governments, as well as companies doing sensitive work with the Defense Department, FBI or CIA.

An Achiever?   Someone who is results-oriented and can get the job done.

A Harmonizer?   Someone who works well with people and will raise morale.

Creativity?   Someone with ideas and a fresh way of approaching problems.

Administrative Skills? Someone who is organized and detail oriented.

Second, answer test questions to fit that particular focus.

Complete these sample items, then read the discussion.

Forced Choice (Circle A or B, that which best describes you.)
1. A. Maintain the status quo.
    B. Encourage change.
2. A. Assign extra work to the most competent.
    B. Assign work equally among team members.
3. A. Dress to fit my taste.
    B. Dress in an acceptable manner.
4. A. Work to accomplish my goals.
    B. Try to reduce tension.
5. A. Emphasize rules and regulations.
    B. Emphasize dealing with people.
6. A. Seek to develop my potential.
    B. Seek to please my boss.
7. A. Uphold standards.
    B. Demonstrate my skills.
8. A. Insist on what is correct.
    B. Look after others' interests.
9. A. People respect me for my competence.
    B. People respect me for the way I deal with them.

10. A. Do things that will pay off.
    B. Take a definite stand on issues.
11. A. Read *Sports Illustrated*.
    B. Read the *Harvard Business Review*.
12. A. I enjoy being with people.
    B. I prefer to read a good book.
13. A. I like to read about crime and murder.
    B. I would like to write a novel.
14. A. Teach engineering.
    B. Teach literature.
15. A. Proceed cautiously.
    B. Take chances.
16. A. Make money.
    B. Make friends.

Yes/No Choice (Circle your preference.)

17. When I believe in something, I never change my mind. (yes/no)
18. Can you work alone? (yes/no)
19. Is any member of your family presently having problems? (yes/no)

Scaled Choices (Check the response that represents your feelings.)

20. I stick to a job until it is done.
__Agree __Probably Agree __Probably Disagree __Disagree
21. Feelings are more important than finishing a project on time.
__Agree __Probably Agree __Probably Disagree __Disagree
22. I sometimes avoid taking a stand that would create controversy.
__Agree __Probably Agree __Probably Disagree __Disagree

23.   Do your feelings shift from happiness to sadness with no
      apparent reason?
__Always   __Usually   __Sometimes   __Rarely   __Never
24.   Place a check in the space that indicates your reaction
to organizational rules and policies:

Active   Passive

Bitter   Sweet

Beautiful   Ugly

Valuable   Worthless

In the next two examples you have 7 points to distribute
between the two items, depending on how they fit your style
and preference. The two boxes must total 7.

25.   Showing I like my customers.   [   ]
      Solving tough problems.   [   ]
26.   Rude—Insensitive.   [   ]
      Ineffective—Useless.   [   ]

Semantic Preference (Check those adjectives that best describe you.)

__angry   __clean
__calm   __discouraged
__friendly   __agreeable
__free   __fun-loving
__nervous   __serious
__cooperative   __impartial

___outgoing	___strong-willed
___reserved	___courteous
___afraid	___cautious
___active	

Discussion of the Sample Test Items

1. *B*. Though I advocate moderation when interviewing, this is not an interview, it's a test, so score *B* as the acceptable answer.

2. *B*. In practice, though, we tend to overload our most competent employees.

3. *B*. But you knew that from Principle 2.

4. *B*. Unless the position calls for working on your own without supervision, e.g., research, sales in a large remote territory.

5. *B*. The recommended choice.

6. *A*. Once on the job, you better please your boss first.

7. *A*. Employers like that.

8. *B*. You can't lose with this answer.

9. *A*. If a technical job.
   B. For most other postions.

10. *A*. *Payoff* is a revered word in business lexicons.

11. *B*. Appear literate.

12. *A*. Hermits and bookworms have difficulty getting jobs.

13. *B*. Unless you want them to think you're a potential serial killer.

14. *A*. If that's what the job calls for.
    B. If the requirements lean more toward creativity, e.g., publishing, advertising and promotion.

15. *A*. The safest answer, unless they're looking for a leader, someone to take charge and turn things around.

16. *B*. The acceptable response, though in reality money is a driving force.

17. *No*. Never say *never*. A *yes* would be interpreted as a rigid person.

18. *Yes*. Suggests you are self-motivated and can accomplish tasks on your own.

19. *No*. None of their business. They would read too much into a *yes*.

On scaled choices like 20–24 avoid checking either end of the scale, except where the behavior is an obvious asset. Extreme responses carry too much weight in the scoring.

20. *Agree*. You can't go wrong on this one.

21. *Probably Disagree*. Even though employers give lip service to caring for others, do your job first. That's what you'll be rewarded for.

22. *Probably Agree*. The safest response. *Disagree* would suggest a troublemaker.

23. *Never*. Though shifts in mood happen to all of us, don't state that here. Your admission would be given too much emphasis by the testers.

24. Lean toward *Active, Sweet, Beautiful, Valuable*.

		X					
Active							Passive

					X		
Bitter							Sweet

```
|_____|_____|___X__|_____|_____|_____|
Beautiful                                   Ugly
|_____|___X__|_____|_____|_____|_____|
Valuable                              Worthless
```

Rules and regulations are an uneasy necessity in organization life. The same holds for 25–26: avoid extreme scores (6–1 or 1–6). They will distort the final assessment.

25. *Customers* [5] If you're going to have a lot of con-
     Problems [2] tact with customers. If not, score
                     5–2 for problem-solving.

26. Rude . . . [4] Sometimes you will face a choice of
     . . . Useless [3] two negatives. Pick the lesser of two
                     evils. In this case "insensitivity" is
                     less objectionable than "useless."

Semantic Preference: Check *calm, friendly, free, cooperative, outgoing, active, clean, agreeable, serious, impartial, courteous.* Avoid negative adjectives.

I repeat: Don't submit to tests if at all possible, but you may find an attractive job that requires testing. If so, follow these guidelines:

- Avoid extreme scores, unless the behavior is an obvious positive from an employer's standpoint.
- Be consistent. Many tests have built-in lie detectors by repeating questions in a slightly different form. Once you decide on an approach, stick to it.

- The more controversial the item, the more you should score it toward the center of the scale.
- Don't admit to any neurotic or deviant behavior.
- When in doubt, give socially acceptable answers, following the Golden Rule and love-thy-neighbor approach.

So much for Truth and Morality and Honesty in the Interview. Remember: Humankind is capable of misusing truth as easily as falsehood.

The simple truth is: We lie. All of us. Every day. We lie consciously and unconsciously, subtly and bluntly, harmfully and harmlessly, by commission and by omission. We lie to survive. We lie because we cannot know all the truth all the time.

Almost always truth comes in shades. *Yes* and *No* responses contain an element of lying for what they leave out.

Even though interviewers say they look for honesty and encourage you to speak out, keep in mind the lessons of King Lear. He and the Earl of Gloucester banished Cordelia, Kent and Edgar for speaking "what we feel, not what we ought."

Satchel Paige's mother advised, "If you tell a lie, always rehearse it. If it don't sound good to you, it won't sound good to anybody else." An aspiring sales rep rationalized one job rejection this way: "I lied about my field experience, but I guess I didn't lie good enough!"

Every life needs a cover story. Edit yours carefully. Latch the gate so the black cats[15] don't get out.

---

[15]Your idiosyncrasies, limitations and failures, which feed on the biases and "superstitions" of interviewers and ultimately eliminate you from consideration.

.   .   .

> AXIOM: Honesty is the key to successful interviewing.
> COROLLARY: Once you've learned to fake that, you've
> got it made.

.   .   .

In Blake Edwards's movie *Sunset*, an aging Wyatt Earp goes to Hollywood to consult on a Wild West film. When asked if the gunfight scenes were true to life, his reply aptly summarizes this chapter:

> "That's the way it happened,
> give or take a lie or two."

TIPS

- Recognize the dangers of total honesty.
- Make sure the interviewer can tolerate candor.
- When asked, inflate your current salary.
- Avoid standing on controversy (e.g., political causes, abortion, environment, conservative versus liberal issues).
- If your lifestyle differs from the norm, keep it to yourself.
- Don't admit to personal problems.
- Throughout the interview slant information in your favor.

PRINCIPLE 5.
ACCENTUATE THE
POSITIVE, ELIMINATE
THE NEGATIVE

• • •

The evil that men do lives after them,
The good is oft interred with their bones.
—Shakespeare, Julius Caesar

Learn it fast, learn it now. The interview is not a confession,
a telltale event. It's a slalom—one miss, one knocked-down
gate, and you're out of the running.

Research demonstrates that negative information introduced early in the interview produces a reject slip. Interviewing is a blackballing process that allows no room for
seepage. Getting through is a matter of *not being disquali-
fied*.

Interviewers candle. Candling is the procedure of moving
eggs across a large light so QC (Quality Control) can detect
cracks or irregularities. Interviewers spotlight you and look
for kinks in your armor (Myth #9 in Part One).

.   .   .

Interviewers do not qualify you; they hire by elimination.

.   .   .

Consider these statements taken from the transcripts of two different interviews:

- "I was fired because my boss was jealous of my accomplishments."
- "Work isn't everything. I have many outside interests I want to pursue."

As you might guess the two applicants were not hired. Each introduced a fact, innocent enough, true enough, that created an element of suspicion about stability and commitment. In a matter of seconds, a promising opportunity ruined.

Another excerpt from an interview:

| Interviewer: | "Tell me something about yourself." |
| Applicant: | "Well, I was born and raised in Rivertown. Never left home until I went to college. Didn't like much about high school. The teachers were aloof and the courses were boring. College wasn't much better. A lot of busywork, and |

I've never been much for homework. Then I took off for a few years. Finally got a job with ISI in sales. The customers weren't very smart, so making quotas was a snap. I left because of management. I don't have a job right now. That's why I'm interviewing with you. Can you tell me something about your company? I've never heard of it before."

These were actual responses; I've compressed them for impact. You should easily identify at least half a dozen "rumblestrips," those speed bumps that warn interviewers to slow down—danger ahead.

For example:

- "Never left home"—Ah-hah, a local. Narrow in thinking, doesn't know anything beyond Rivertown.
- "Never much for homework"—Lazy, not a hard worker.
- "Customers weren't very smart"—A know-it-all, will appear arrogant and turn off customers.
- "I've never heard of it [your company] before"— Whatta loser. We're a first-rate business and he never even looked us up.

Not to mention the unsaid thoughts following three truncated statements:

- "I took off a few years . . ."
- "I left because of management . . ."
- "I don't have a job right now . . ."

Hmm, I wonder why?

These are dangerous for what they leave out, prompting the interviewer to speculate sinister causes.

The theme of this chapter is that you must avoid hemlock remarks that poison the interviewer's perception of you. You can accomplish this by:

- Accentuating the positive
- Eliminating the negative
- Turning potential negatives into positives

Accentuating the Positive

Positioning yourself for employment is the closest you will come to perfection until your obituary. So prepare a panoply of accomplishments, an impressive array of traits and experiences appropriate to each job.

You bring a dowry of talent to any organization. Package it well and be proud of it. Focusing on positives leaves little room for dwelling on negatives.

In the left-hand column on the next page, list your personal and professional accomplishments and qualities. (Refer to Principle 2 and Principle 3 for the attributes that make interviewers smile.) In the right-hand column note how they apply to the job for which you are interviewing.

You cannot relate all achievements to every position. Part of your assignment is to decide which will have the greatest

Accentuate the Positives

Positives	Application to This Job
I. Accomplishments & Awards A. On the Job	
B. In School	
C. In Family & Community	
II. Personal & Professional Strengths	

impact. For instance, a master's degree could be a deficit in applying for "plant supervisor," but a project in which you directed the activities of five others would be a definite asset. Or pushing burgers for McDonald's might not contribute to that secretary's job, but "helping the store manager organize the beginning of each day" would be a big plus.

For the proper frame of mind you need to have *la vista gorda* (large vision), attributed to Spanish wives who overlook their husbands' philandering. Become so involved in drawing your many dimensions that you don't let limitations affect confidence in the interview.

If you were applying for the Marketing Assistant position on page 115, "Accentuating the Positives" might look something like this:

IA. Job Accomplishments/ Awards	Job Description
Letter of commendation on the QC Task Force project for:	
• Researching how other companies are promoting quality	• 1e. Marketing research
• Coordinating the schedules of Task Force members	• 3 & 6. Liaison with sales & others
• Keeping accurate minutes	• 1. Administration
• Following through on assignments	• 4 & 5. Contact product managers and update policies
• "Excellent" rating on most recent performance appraisal, which noted the thoroughness and timeliness of my reports	• 1b. Rendering reports

**IB. School Accomplish-
ments/Awards**

- Honor roll   8. Potential for other activities
- Minor in communications   1c. Communicating
- Treasurer of Kappa Alpha   1a & 7. Budgeting
  Theta

IC. Family/Community

- Design and print our annual Christmas cards   7. Working with outside services (art)
- Keep attendance records for the church and follow up when needed   1. Administration

II. Personal/Professional

- Good organizer   1. Administration
- Make friends easily   3, 4 & 6. Coordinating through others
- Handle pressure without losing my cool   1d & 2. Answering telephone inquiries and complaints

One more accent on the affirmative: Make sure you can recite some positives about the organization for which you would like to work, such as:

- Its reputation
- People in the organization whom you respect
- Recent growth
- Its most successful product or service
- A particularly clever or humorous company advertisement

- Societal contributions (environment, charities, foundation activities)
- Attractiveness of brochures or annual report
- Architecture of the corporate headquarters

Eliminating the Negative

Someone once described a general as "better at avoiding disaster than achieving brilliant victories." Not a bad model for interviewing.

If you want your interview to develop a Titanic tilt, discuss your faults and failings. Since that's not your objective, begin

by fumigating your past of those pesky experiences and notions that eliminate you from consideration.

What are they? Here is a list of potential disasters, irretrievable moments that turn off prospective employers. A few have been mentioned before but deserve repeating here.

- Failure to fill in all blanks on the application—will create suspicion[16]
- A smudgy, sloppily completed application that looks like a Rorschach
- Years missing in your work history—another red flag
- Showing up late for the interview
- Being unemployed at the time of the interview raises eyebrows (unless, of course, you're fresh out of college). Nobody in his or her right mind would quit before finding another job. Who's going to pay the mortgage?
- Unkempt appearance
- Poor scholastic record
- Willing to take less money than your previous job—gives the impression of desperation
- Reluctance to get your hands dirty—every job, no matter what level, has its scut and scrub work. Interviewers like to feel you understand and appreciate this.
- A limp handshake
- Lack of confidence—preparation and practice overcome self-doubt.
- Appearing to be a know-it-all

---

[16]Some employment forms ask questions that could become Equal Employment Opportunity issues. See Appendix A for a discussion of these.

- Admitting you didn't work out on a previous job. No matter what reason, where there's smoke there's fire.
- No sense of humor
- Lack of knowledge in your field of concentration
- Failure to get along with superiors or colleagues
- Unwilling to accept criticism—you will be unmanageable
- Unenthusiastic style
- Lack of courtesy
- Knocking previous employers and colleagues—"If you're critical of them, you'll be critical of us."
- Poor eye contact—you must be hiding something or are too timid for this job.
- Unclear responses to questions
- Radical ideas
- Refusal to relocate—employers don't take kindly to this. It suggests you're inflexible and may be a problem at some later date.
- Objecting to travel—same as above
- Immaturity
- Health problems
- Financial irresponsibility
- No career plan—you don't seem to know where you're going.
- Failure to show interest in the organization

Whitewash your past of these blemishes. Run your affairs through a mental Laundromat to eliminate dirty linen.

There is no undoing in the interview. If you're unemployed,

don't mention it. If you've ever been fired, don't mention it. If you didn't get along with your last supervisor, don't mention it. If your current salary is much lower than what you are asking, don't mention it. Can interviewers check on such information? Not likely. Insist that your "current" employer not be contacted. That is accepted practice in the employment arena.

.   .   .

RULE OF THUMB: It takes twenty accomplishments to undo one mistake.

.   .   .

Turn Negatives into Positives

Only the gods are spotless. We mortals must live with our shortfalls. Most stains we can launder, but some are irremovable and obvious to all (e.g., low grade-point average, uneven job history). A savvy person learns how to take advantage of limitations.

Ready yourself for questions like:

- What do you consider some of your weaknesses?
- What about your grades?
- Why have you had four jobs in three years?
- I notice you don't have any selling experience.
- Are you willing to take a pay cut? (Could be asked if your stated salary is above the maximum offered, or the interviewer might just be testing you.)

- Where is Winset College?
- Why do you want to leave your current position?

Anticipate your "Achilles' heel" with thought-through answers. Learn how to:

Disguise—Just as makeup can hide zits, we can obscure the existence of real or perceived blemishes in personality and work history.

Camouflage—A form of disguise in which you cause the interviewer to overlook something in your background.

Distract—Draw the interviewer's attention away from a potentially damaging subject by asking a question.

Divert—Deflect an issue toward another course, like interesting a child in a toy when she really wants to play with the crystal.

If every cloud has a silver lining, perhaps every negative has a positive side. Below and on the following pages I detail some transitions from weakness to strength, from questionable to definite asset, by disguising, camouflaging, distracting and diverting.

Apparent Weakness	Slanted to a Strength
Frequent job-changing	"My objective has been to get a wide variety of experience. Each job I've had has introduced me to a different aspect of the business world. At Trace it was administration; at ISI, sales; and at MPI, marketing and promotion."

Apparent Weakness	Slanted to a Strength
Two blank years in your work history (beachcombing)	"In 1990 I took two years off to better understand the country. Traveled twenty-four states. It also gave me a chance to step back and re-define my career goals." (Be prepared to state them.)
Too task-oriented	"I'm like a pit bull. When I take hold of an assignment, I don't let go until it's done."
Low-to-average grades	"I tried to involve myself in as many activities as I could and learned a lot from them. I sang in the choir, partici-pated in student government, lettered in soccer, wrote for the school newspaper, and was counselor in the freshmen dorm. I know this stole some time from strictly 'book learning,' but was valuable nonetheless."
Lapse in memory	If obvious: "I just don't re-member that. I know five min-utes after I leave here it will come to me."
	If not obvious: Divert to a re-lated topic and go on. For in-

Apparent Weakness	Slanted to a Strength
	stance, the interviewer asks, "What three professors had the most influence on you?" You go blank. Start talking about the class you liked best. "Well, economics was tremendous. He related concepts to what was happening on campus, we had a chance to debate issues, and . . ."
A question you can't answer	If obvious: "I really don't know the answer to that." (nondefensive)
	If not obvious: Disguise by answering a twin question à la tactics used by politicians. For example, the interviewer asks, "Why do you think retail discount store sales are dwindling?" Daaw, you don't know. Start on customer service: "I don't think we treat customers right. We give lip service, but in practice don't trust them, don't pay enough attention to them, and . . ."
Lack of experience	"It's not the quantity of experience, it's the quality. One summer I participated in

Apparent Weakness	Slanted to a Strength
	a mock-government experiment. We campaigned, promoted, elected representatives, and passed legislation. I learned more about government in one month than all my schooling put together. Plus the nice thing about experience is: Each day I gain a little more."
Taking a cut in pay (You need the job.)	"I'm at a stage in my life where I'm more interested in opportunity than pay. That doesn't mean I don't value salary, but at the moment I want a position where I can grow and advance."
Age[17]	If too young: Underline your energy, enthusiasm and eagerness to learn. If over forty: Line up a series of work successes to show your depth and breadth of knowledge.

[17]Age is another Equal Employment Opportunity no-no, yet employers still ask directly or indirectly. Again, refer to EEO considerations in Appendix A.

Apparent Weakness	Slanted to a Strength
On being fired	If for some reason you go public: "I was RIF-ed. [That's the government term for Reduction In Force.] Because of the recent recession, my unit was eliminated as part of a massive cutback plan."
On being unemployed before you've secured another job	If not asked directly ("Where are you working now?"): Don't bring up the subject.
	If asked directly and you've been unemployed under six months: "I'm on severance pay, which gives me time to make this transition."
	If more than six months: "I've been doing telecommunications part time [or some other job you've worked at] and taking a career planning workshop at the community college."
Education from a small, lesser known college	"I'm glad I went to Winset College. Because it was small I had a chance to interact with professors in and out of class, and to assume leader-

Apparent Weakness	Slanted to a Strength
	ship in a variety of extracurricular activities." (Cite one or two that you can talk about easily.)
Working for an obscure, non-prestigious company	"I know ISI is not a Fortune 500 company, but in a way I get more attention and have worked in three different departments. The hands-on experience has been fantastic."

Of course, you cannot take these suggestions verbatim. Standing alone, any one might seem hokey, unrealistic or even laughable. They are directional and meant to trigger answers of your own.

Don't let inadequacies color your view of the interview. Have faith in yourself, and with gall and guile sell that faith.

"What's past is prologue" (Shakespeare), so deep-six any eyebrow-raisers. Avoid the kerfs in your past. Carpenters know what I'm talking about. Kerfs are unwanted slits in wood, which, as you saw, get bigger and bigger until the board splits in two.

Unless you welcome a flood of rejects, "accentuate the positive and eliminate the negative." This principle is crucial to passing muster, and it's not a bad philosophy of life.

REMEMBER: If you think ill of yourself,
                  If you fret your limitations,
                  If you act unsure of your ability to deliver,
                  So will the interviewer.

TIPS

DO:

- Pan your waters for gold.
- Tout your talents.
- Camouflage failure.
- Prepare explanations for weak spots.
- Complete all applications in full.
- Be flexible on starting dates.
- Present yourself in the best light.
- Highlight your vastness.

DON'T:

- Admit you've been fired.
- Let on you did not get along with superiors, no matter how incompetent they were.
- Mention that your favorite book was Kitty Kelley's 1991 tittle-tattler *Nancy Reagan, The Unauthorized Biography* or Derek Humphrey's case for suicide in *Final Exit.*
- Smoke or chew.
- Act superior, even if you are.
- Confess you were kicked out of the Boy or Girl Scouts.
- Monopolize the conversation.
- Disagree with or nettle the interviewer.
- Talk about your role in student sit-ins.
- Intimate that you can only work nine to five.

- Describe the time you had too much road sauce and barfed all over a Joan of Arc statue in the town square.
- Say, "I'm just shopping around."

     •   •   •

> Approach the interview as a celebration of you and of possibility.

     •   •   •

PRINCIPLE 6. SAY IT LIGHT AND SAY IT BRIGHT

• • •

For by thy words thou shalt be justified,
and by thy words thou shalt be condemned.
—Matthew 12:37

At the beginning of his course one of my college professors distributed a mimeographed booklet he had written entitled "Write It Right and Brightly." It emphasized using words accurately and actively.

Principle 6 takes up this notion, and for good cause. The main reason recruiters say they reject college students is *poor communication skills*. Western culture values verbal ability. SATs and other standardized tests favor students with expansive vocabularies who speak and write fluently. We infer intelligence from the way people express themselves.

• • •

How you say it is as important as what you say.

• • •

In this chapter I will:

- State some generalizations about communicating
- Define communication as used here
- Look at blocks to communicating in the interview
- Outline guidelines for saying it lightly and brightly

Generalizations

By "generalization" I mean a statement about human interaction that is more often true than false. The following generalizations lay a foundation for the ideas and suggestions in this chapter:

1. Speech is a metaphor for the world, not the world itself, and, therefore, open to misinterpretation.

2. In all communication a natural gap exists between speaker and audience.

3. There is no such thing as "no communication" in interpersonal dealings. We are always communicating, even when no words are exchanged.

4. Most communication mishaps are caused by too much information, not too little.

5. We seldom communicate what we mean.

6. Meaning is in the ear of the receiver.

7. In interviewing naturalness is all—any communication technique must be within your natural leanings.

8. Presentation : Message :: Music : Lyrics.

What Is Communication?

Somebody has estimated that we communicate 75 percent of our waking hours. Approximately one third of that time we speak and one half we listen. If those estimates are anywhere near accurate, one half of each year is consumed by some communication activity. Another way of looking at it is that you have accumulated at least ten years of experience in communicating by the time you interview for your first job.

The aim of this chapter is to improve the quality of that experience as it relates to job-getting.

By communication I mean:

An exchange of facts and feelings
that forms a connection between two or more persons.

The key words are *exchange, feelings, connection*. All exchanges have an emotional component as well as informational. "Nice job" seems like a simple statement of recognition, clear enough, but the intonation might send a different message, e.g., a backhanded compliment connoting sarcasm, insincerity, jealousy.

The exchange must produce a connection. Communication is like a forward pass in football. No matter how accurate and how beautiful a spiral, it's not complete until caught by the receiver.

Connections are necessary because a gap exists between any two persons, even friends. The distance between you and interviewers is sizable. For one, you are strangers. Two, the interview is a strained form of human interaction, not based on parity. Three, both parties feel the stress of having to succeed.

The classic view of communication—sender, receiver and message—omits the concept of gaps. The responsibility for bridging gaps in the interview is yours. The tool for bridging is communication. Let's look at blockages (gap extenders) and what you can do to create connections.

Blocks to Communication

Like a mine field the interview is laden with communication traps. Here are the major ones:

Alligator Words

Don't try to make an impression with a stretched-out vocabulary. You may end up in the swamp they came from, because interviewers suffer from floccinaucinihilipilification.[18]

You see, sesquipedalianism obfuscates the interface and generates disapprobation and ostracism!

Clear enough?

Pat Phrases

Most clichés imply shallowness and turn off interviewers. Some examples:

- "Run it up the flagpole and see which way the wind blows."

[18]The longest word in the unabridged *Oxford English Dictionary*, meaning "considering something worthless if you don't agree with or understand it."

- "Let sleeping dogs lie."
- "That's the way the cookie crumbles."
- "It's Greek to me."
- "Variety's the spice of life."
- "Beauty is only skin deep."
- "It is better to give than to receive."
- "Half a loaf is better than none."
- "The problem is communication."

Avoid using phrases that have been repeated so often they get in the way rather than contribute to understanding.

Information Overkill

This is the age of the knowledge mushroom and mass media massage. Every day we are bombarded by news and analysis upon analysis—TV, radio, books, magazines, newspapers, and mail we didn't ask for. The problem is how to sort through these transmissions for dispatches that are useful and manageable.

The interview occurs against this backdrop. If you load interviewers with facts and figures, they will do what I did with my college notes: label, box, bury.

A Deaf Ear

Wearing earplugs means missing half the message. Failure to listen results in interruptions and missed cues. Failure to listen leads to an "F" in Communications.

Confirming the Obvious

"Of course, it's obvious" means any dummy (like the interviewer) should know that. Whiteout those words from your script. Nothing is obvious if you haven't encountered it before. Keep in mind the Will Rogers rejoiner: "Everyone is ignorant, only on different subjects."

Understatement

Too little information is as harmful as too much, because interviewers may think your knowledge is superficial, and you don't have any ideas.

.   .   .

```
Neither a clam nor clapper-jaw be.
```

.   .   .

Arguing or Persuading

Don't enter a taffy pull with interviewers. Trying to debate or convince them your viewpoint is right will earn only demerits.

Gaffes[19]

Blunders, slips of the tongue, don't help your cause. In Yiddish the word for it is *"fumfur"*: people who chatter through their noses or trip over their tongues and don't know what they're talking about. *Fumfurs* don't pass the interview.

If you commit a faux pas, like a comedian have a retort at the ready, and rather than self-consciously cover it up, be prepared to laugh at yourself.

Stammering

Usually punctuated with a nervous "ah," "er," "umm," or a throat-clearing "harrumph," giving hints of insecurity and indecision.

The Greenhouse Effect

The warming of the interview room caused by an increase in carbon dioxide produced by burning fossil thoughts. The effect might be described as woolliness. One can argue a fair case that

$$fuzzy\ expression = fuzzy\ thinking$$

Woolly conversation usually takes the form of unfinished statements, generalities, hackneyed phrases, failure to answer

[19]Journalists in Washington, D.C., run a gaffe meter on politicians. Former President Ford registered high on the meter; Lloyd Bentsen, Michael Dukakis's vice-presidential running mate in 1988, scored low.

the question, and recycling topics without reaching conclusions. Ask a woolly question and get a woolly answer, like an examination question from my college philosophy professor: "Discuss the universe and give three examples."

Here's the Greenhouse Effect at work in an interview:

INTERVIEWER: "What do you mean by 'adequate'?"
CANDIDATE: "The performance of most people is adequate."
INTERVIEWER: "What do you mean by 'adequate'?"
C: "Adequate is like . . . ah . . . well, how can you explain it? It's what a lot of people are. You know, Mary had an adequate year."
I: "You mean just an average employee?"
C: "Well, you know, meeting a standard . . . meeting a standard."
I: "You mean not doing anything that is different or better?"
C: "Well, I think we all do individual things that . . . er . . . contribute to how we do our job."
I: "I'm still not clear what you mean."
C: "You know, the company had an adequate year, employees have adequate years. . . ."
I: "Hmm . . ."

Now we know what "adequate" is. Hmm . . .

Foghorn Dialogue

Wording that warns the interviewer your ship is headed for the shoals. For example:

- "Everything's fine."
- "I can't think of any weaknesses."
- "I love to work with people." (Who else, chimpanzees?)
- "I don't have any questions."
- "How much vacation do I get the first year?"

Semantics

Assuming meaning is in the word, when it's actually in the heads and minds of those dialoguing. Imagine, for instance, the possibilities of interpretation in words like *conservative, liberal, Democrat, Republican, capitalist, commie*[20], *radical, faggot, Nazi, garbage collector, abortion, hawk, environmentalism, ghetto, feminist, labor unions, welfare, bag lady, autocratic manager, peaceniks, loyalty, patriotism.*

Value-laden terms muddy the streams of communication. Failure to be specific can produce gross misunderstandings in the interview.

"Speak Loud Here, Logic Weak" Syndrome

That bit of advice was written in the margin of a sermon by my peripatetic Methodist minister uncle. He serviced small

---

[20]A comedian satirized the semantic issue when he defined the difference between communism and capitalism: "In communism, man uses man. With capitalism it's just the other way around."

WISHFUL THINKING IN THE MIDDLE EAST.

churches in the Adirondack Mountains, churches that could not afford a full-time minister. For three summers I rode with him as he made the rounds from parish to parish. This note was obviously a tongue-in-cheek remark, but some people do operate at loudspeaker levels, and usually the decibels relate inversely to the rationality of their discourse. You cannot megaphone your way to a job.

Using Any of Four Voices

Superiority: "Those people down there just don't understand what I'm saying. They can't possibility know what it's like up here making decisions. That's why there are so many problems down on the assembly line. They don't have our perspective."

Suspicion: "Why do you want to know that? I don't think what I do in my spare time relates to this job. What are you getting at?"

Rigidity: "That's the way you sell health-care products. That's the way it's always been. I don't see any reason to change."

Indifference: "I guess so, whatever you say." Or no response except a shrug of the shoulders, like my teenager when I ask, "What are you going to do tonight?"

These four voices will prevent you from connecting with interviewers.

Verbal mishaps—*blocks*, I call them—lead to four communication outlaws:

- Redundancy
- Gibberish
- Confusion
- A lackluster presentation

They are outlaws because they steal your chance for a job.

All of us set up one or more roadblocks daily. If your objective is to scramble communications, to create static, then become a professional blocker. Since, as a job hunter, that is not your aim, the second half of this chapter addresses ways to bridge the interviewing gap.

Guidelines for Saying It Lightly and Brightly

1. Unblock.

Many obstacles can interfere, not the least of which are the blocks listed on previous pages. *Remove them*. Don't let them stand in the way of your job. Unblock from:

- Annoying verbal and nonverbal habits.
- Lack of things to say, by preplanning.
- Fear of failure. Remember, even if you're not hired, each interview becomes a learning experience for the next.
- Awe of authority. No matter what rank the interviewer, you are assessing the organization as well as being evaluated.
- Stress in the environment. Most settings are not conducive to dialogue—a desk in a gray room with a total lack of ambience. Focus on your performance. I suppose it's like a concert recital—barren stage, bright lights and a house full of critics. The artist thinks only of the next piece. Like that artist, concentrate on yourself, front and center, and stress will become part of the backdrop.
- Knowledge of your inadequacies. Each of us has them, so big deal. And you're the only one in the room who knows what they are.

2. Rehearse.

Principle 1 discussed the importance of practice. Assemble answers to the most often asked questions (see Appendix B) and rehearse explaining weaknesses in your personal and professional background.

Prepare ad-libs—even Johnny Carson does that. For instance, I use a Mark Twain quip when I misspell a word writing in front of a group: "I don't think much of a man who can only figure out one way to spell a word."

Ready your initial approach to the interviewer and the interview.

3. Use Sound Bites.

Those snippets of videotape that catch the highlights of an event, a speech, a product. Contemporary culture has evolved to the point where if ideas don't fit on a T-shirt or bumper sticker, they aren't of worth.

At cocktail parties I've resorted to telling people that "I make a fine brand of foot powder." Why? Because the asker really doesn't wish a dissertation on what I do. He or she just wants to know am I a mechanic, teacher, accountant, doctor. Anything more produces fidgeting, looking around, and finally a polite, "Excuse me, I need to get a refill."

Come to the point. Let interviewers indicate if they want to know more.

4. Be Obsessed with Clarity.

To promote clarity:

- Develop your interplan (page 61).
- Write out key points you want to emphasize.

- Specify what features and benefits the organization will accrue if you come aboard.

- Show rather than tell, using copious examples to link your ideas to the work world.

- On key issues: State your position.
  Develop it.
  Restate it.
  An age-old formula but still effective.

5. Make the Most of Picturesque Speech.

Trade on metaphors to charge your expression. (After all, what is "meta for?"). In an April 1991 *Sports Illustrated* article on the Evander Holyfield–George Foreman heavyweight championship fight, Pat Putnam described it in these terms:

- ". . . an F–15 versus a Goodyear blimp."

- "Foreman came out of Houston, Texas, with a dream. For 36 minutes he was Holyfield's nightmare."

- "Holyfield was champion of the WBA, IBF, and WBC; Foreman was champion of the AARP."

- ". . . you could time his [Foreman's] punches with a sundial."

Employ tiger verbs and nouns—words that spring at interviewers and get their attention. If you backpedal over the last twenty pages, you will notice attempts at sprightliness. I recall a wonderful Thoreau description from high school English that went something like this: "The tanager flew through the foliage as if to *ignite* the leaves." A lively association with the scarlet color of the bird. I'm not suggesting you become a poet, but two or three fresh-ground phrases in an interview can percolate an unforgettable brew.

6. Listen.

When we're not sending messages, we're receiving. Most of us espouse active listening but few practice it. Walk through any office or plant and it's a rarity to see a boss listening to employees. In the experiment mentioned in Part One (Myth #6), I found interviewers aren't so hot either. They tend to patter on, leaving only one fourth of the discourse for potential listening.[21]

Some listening tips:

- Plan pauses to take mental stock of the situation.[22]
- Hear feelings as well as facts.
- Ask questions to clarify, e.g., "Could you expand on that?" or "How do you mean that?"
- Restate complex points to get the interviewer's confirmation that you are on the right track.
- Be attentive to interviewers instead of mulling over your next answer.

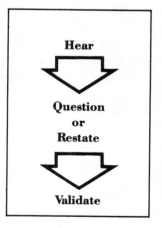

[21]This raises an interesting question: When are interviewers gathering the facts necessary to make informed decisions? The data support an earlier notion that they decide early in the interview based on one or two observations, then use the remaining time to justify their judgments.

[22]Oliver Wendell Holmes said, "Talking is like playing the harp; there is as much in laying the hands on the strings to stop their vibrations as in twanging them to bring out their music."

Active listening is not a natural process. Our minds cruise five times faster than our mouths. Listening requires energy and system. It is hard work, but pays big dividends.

In 1980 Sperry Corporation recognized these dividends when it ran a multimillion-dollar advertising campaign with the slogan "We understand how important it is to listen." The ad went on: "We've recently set up special listening programs that Sperry personnel worldwide can attend. And what we're discovering is that when people really know how to listen they can actually encourage the speakers to share more of their thoughts and feelings, bringing everyone closer together. Which is of great value to us when we do business. And perhaps even greater value when we are home."

In Tom Peters's handbook for a management revolution, *Thriving on Chaos*, listening is indexed twenty-eight times and is cited as a key leadership skill.

Don't underestimate the power of paying attention. Following the above suggestions for active listening increases the accuracy of information, minimizes disagreement, ensures you are responding to what is being asked and lends an aura of caring about the interviewer and the organization.

7. Vary Tone, Inflection, Pitch, Volume.

Don't metronome your words in undisturbed staccato tones. Find your voice. Give variety to it. Listen to your tape recordings to identify speech mannerisms that grate on the interviewer—too high pitched, too loud or soft, a monotone, a bland, singsong delivery. Most of us are not blessed with the barrel tones of James Earl Jones. Most of us lack *squillo*

(Italian for ringping in a voice à la Pavarotti), but we can deliver our messages within an acceptable range.

Ask a close friend to critique the way you sound. Try a speech class or elocution lessons. (If three-hundred-pound football players can dance ballet, why not?)

8. When in Doubt, Mumble?

No, not really. That's the title of a delightful book by James H. Boren (Van Nostrand Reinhold Company, 1972). Instead:

- When in doubt, take a deep breath—from the diaphragm, of course, unnoticed by the audience.
- When in doubt, ask a question—to regroup, to buy thinking time, to seek more information.
- When in doubt, try "et cetera"—that makes it sound like you have much more to voice, when in fact you've exhausted all thinking on the matter.

9. Watch Your Nonverbals.

I read where researchers at the University of Iowa are training pigeons to decipher the meaning behind certain human facial expressions. My Irish wolfhound puppy doesn't understand my prattling, but she reads every movement, smile, grimace, frown, question mark, even my silences. Though much of communication is nonverbal, I approach the subject cautiously. Like dreams, body language is difficult to read and lends itself to various interpretations. Nevertheless, the next pages list some obvious do's and don't's.

Nonverbal Communication	Interviewer's Likely Inference
Nose in the air	Superiority
Picking your nose	Ugh!
Thumbing your nose	And the same to you
Thumbs down	Reject
Raised eyebrow	Suspicion
Head bowed	Submission
Hands clenched	Tension
Arms akimbo	You disapprove
Arms crossed on chest	Closed mind
Clenched teeth	Anger
Chewing gum	A slob
Tapping feet/fingers/pencil	Restlessness
Yawning	You're tired or bored.
Slumping in your chair	Lethargy
Biting your nails	Nervousness
Nodding your head horizontally	You disagree.
Hemming and hawing	You don't know.
Poor eye contact	You're afraid, unsure.
Wearing dark glasses	You have something to hide.
Limp handshake	Whishy-washy, no conviction
Expressionless	Are you with it?
Firm handshake	Confidence
Smile	Pleasant, cheerful
Direct eye contact	Credible, trustworthy
Head held high	Proud, sure of yourself
Hands, palms up	Openness
Hands, gesticulating	Animated, energetic
Leaning forward	Intimacy
Nodding head vertically	Agreement
Thumbs up	A winner

Avoid the first twenty-one mannerisms, and use the rest freely. Stick to movements that create positive impressions.

In an age of computers, 150-channel televisions, cellular telephones, communications satellites, and digital this and digital that, face-to-face skills are becoming a lost art. We must retrieve them.

Telling your story is selling.

Selling is presenting.

Presenting requires grace and polish.

The way you articulate yourself determines whether the interviewer positions you on the Einstein or Clem Kadiddlehopper side of intelligence. Intent isn't enough. Content isn't enough. Even clarity will not suffice (you can be clear and boring, clear and irrelevant).

If you don't want the interviewer to think someone blew out your pilot light, be a firefly. Luminate.

Say it right!

Say it light!

Say it bright!

.   .   .

How forcible are right words!
—Job 6:25

.   .   .

TIPS

- Keep it simple.
- Remove blocks to communicating.
- Check for understanding.
- Use words in motion.
- Trim away superfluities, inanities, nebulosities.
- Prepare a few chewy nuggets.
- Thou shalt not a mumbler be.
- Thou shalt not a windjammer be.
- Don't tell tales (gossip).
- Avoid utterances like:
    "That's all she wrote."
    "You must understand . . ."
    "You know . . ."
    "To tell the truth . . ."
    "Thing-a-ma-jig."
    "Blah, blah, blah."
- Let your expression do justice to your thoughts. Remember: How smart you are will be gauged by what you say and the way you say it.

PRINCIPLE 7. HOTSHOT FLOOGIE WITH A FLOY FLOY

. . .

When I was a kid looking for a gingerbread house in the woods, knowing I could eat my way to contentment,[23] I recall a catchy tune played on the radio called "Fat Foot Fuggy in a Foy Foy." At least that's the title my child's ear heard. Actually it was "Flat Foot Floogie (with the Floy Floy)." I remember that the song had a standout beat. If you listen to it, I believe that child-ear was correct.

Part of the theme for this chapter was taken from that music. A few years ago I heard an aging jazz performer describe "floy floy" as a special flair that transcends the ordinary.

The other half of the chapter's title comes from a conversation with the president of a franchise. I asked how he recruited successful franchisees. Without hesitation he responded, "I look for a hot pants!" In his autobiography Lee Iacocca referred to "someone with fire in his belly." For

[23]In my teens that fantasy turned toward finding Snow White. Now it's the lottery.

the French it's *"un coup de foudre*," which literally trans-
lates as "the stroke of a thunderbolt."

Interviewers favor swashbucklers, the John Waynes of the
world. Of course, the search for heroes is not limited to interviewers. Note which movies (and their sequels) have been
popular in the late eighties and early nineties. Blockbusters
like *Die Hard, Rambo, Lethal Weapon, Rocky, Indiana
Jones, Star Wars*, and the assorted (or is it sordid?) adventures of Arnold Schwarzenegger.

·   ·   ·

> At all levels interviewers look for leadership qualities.

·   ·   ·

This principle poses a dilemma for women. Do interviewers
value drive and get-up-and-go for females as they do for
males? My answer is yes, but not in the same degree. They're
not looking for Connie the Barbarian. Two 1991 movies in
which women shoot up the place and generally raise hell,
Thelma and Louise and *V. I. Warshawski*, received mixed
reviews. Also, who interviews you makes a difference. In an
age of feminism men are generally uneasy interviewing women.
They're not sure how to behave and what questions to ask.
Conversely, female interviewers tend to be tougher on female
applicants. Regardless of gender, interviewers favor flair. My
advice is that you demonstrate floy floy, but in a lesser degree
than men. Tone it down so as not to disturb the interviewer's
prejudices.

On its face this chapter may appear to contradict the cau-
tion of previous ones. Not really. A Mainer friend tells me
that when fog suddenly sets in, he turns his lobster boat in
circles, creating waves that eventually rock a buoy in the

vicinity, ringing its bell. By making waves he finds his course. He could avoid danger altogether by not launching in the first place, but he realizes a boat in harbor never gets anywhere.

You need to make a ripple or two because interviews are boring. Yes, bor-ing. Dull, dull, dull. When I die I want it to occur in an interview, because then the transition from life to death will be imperceptible.[24]

You should be stable, yes, but not a cardboard pop-up. You won't get picked if you're Dr. Dryasdust, Sir Walter Scott's character in *Ivanhoe* who blathered about dull subjects. Blow one breath of fresh air in the interview, and you leap heads above other candidates. That's the subject of this chapter: How to create floy floy, a kind of go-go leadership, without sounding like an inhabitant of cloud-cuckoo land.

I realize that generating energy in interviews is an abstract principle. Here are some tangible suggestions from my grab bag of ideas.

On Generating Floy Floy in the Interview

Psych Up

Condition yourself mentally and emotionally. Psyching up is usually done the night before, the morning of or while you're in the waiting room. It consists of:

- Cramming
- Perking

---

[24]Since I came to that conclusion, I have added the classroom and staff meetings to the list.

Cramming is the content part of psyching up. I know some teachers argue the negative aspects of cramming, but I think they're wrong. Reviewing bits of relevant information just prior to test time helps recall during the exam. Review your interplan, update yourself with the morning paper headlines and brush up on the job, company products and services.

Perking is the spiritual component. Actors perk before performing the same play and reciting the same lines nine times a week. Supposedly, Tibetan monks chant *"Om"* with such force that their souls fly out the tops of their heads. You need some kind of revving up to loosen up.

Sparking heat into the lukewarm atmosphere of the interview is your responsibility, and yours only. Start the juices flowing. Riding to your appointment, give yourself a chalk talk, hum passionately, sing scales, fill yourself up, put a tiger in your tank. You are the best applicant for the job.

A psyching-up ritual charges your battery. Some wag put it this way: "Try thirty seconds of meditation to clear your head for a minute."

Pinball Ideas

Bounce ideas off the interviewer that ring bells and turn on lights, but never tilt the balance against you. Develop at least one speculation about basic human endeavors such as governing, communicating, transporting, family, leisure, work.

An idea person is an ideal person.

Here are examples of what I mean, some facetious, some serious:

- There are two kinds of events: probables and inevitables. The trick is to recognize the inevitables (foreign competition, scarcity of resources, desegregation) and usher them in in an orderly manner. With probables you have the choice to promote some at the expense of others.

- We need to find novel answers to age-old problems. For example, a promising approach in medicine is to train cancer cells to behave rather than eradicate them. Or in transplants, to disguise cells of the new organ, so the body can't tell they're foreign, hence won't reject them.

- To resolve the oil crisis I suggest we fashion an enormous hollow drill that starts in Seminole, Texas, goes through the earth and comes up under Iraq. Then start suctioning off oil a little at a time.

- I think most organizations suffer from "compartmentalization." Improving cooperation between departments would significantly increase productivity.

- Nothing is inherently wrong with change. It's how we manage it that produces effective or ineffective results.

- There are two kinds of decisions: expensive ones and low-cost ones. Take your time to think through big bucks. The cheapies, decide immediately.

Of course, these observations represent my slant on the world. Parade your own cascade of thoughts. Especially conceive at least one novel way to approach the job for which you are applying.

·   ·   ·

One brainstorm in an interview stands out like the Empire State Building.

·   ·   ·

Hunch a Lot

Hunching is a lost art. It's intuiting, hypothesizing and speculating that "if this is so, then this will happen"—a disarming technique in interviews. Prefacing responses to difficult questions with "My hunch is" suggests a certain humility, a willingness to examine your answer further.

In *The Divine Comedy* Dante wrote about those souls damned because of neutrality: "*Non ragioniam di lor, ma guarda, e passa.*" ("Let us not speak of them; but look, and pass on.") A noncommittal candidate comes off as a weakling, and most interviewers will pass on. Hunching allows you to take a stand in shifting sand rather than concrete—e.g., "My hunch is, if we listened to customers we would sell twice as many cars." A strong statement, but notice it permits wiggle room in case the interviewer disagrees with your point of view.

Draw Tangents

The Greek poet Archilochus wrote, "The fox knows many things, but the hedgehog knows one big thing." As with any parable, interpretations abound. One is the generalist versus specialist, with the latter triumphing. In interviewing I believe the fox "generally" wins out. I'm not talking about training and qualifications for a highly technical job such as a nuclear physicist, but rather your performance in the interview.

Tangents, parenthetical expressions, give the impression of divergent thinking, of breadth of knowledge. For instance, most of the footnotes in this book are asides, tangential to the main thought, rather than a documentation of sources. You may choose to read them or not. They are meant to add interest and relate to other areas of living.

When the discussion triggers a personal experience, go for it, as long as you come back to the original topic.

INTERVIEWER: "We have a task force studying how we can increase sales."

INTERVIEWEE: "Last weekend we were having dinner in the Brass Rail. I ordered roast beef and baked potato. The waitress brought French fries. When I complained, she said they didn't have baked. I suggested she might have come over and asked me if I preferred a substitute. Her reply, 'Oh, well, it wouldn't have made a difference, fries are all we have.' Add to this rudeness slow service and high prices, and you have two disgruntled diners. My point is, I think too often we leave our servers out of the equation—those people who come in contact with customers. They should be selected more carefully and trained in interpersonal relations. Their behavior impacts sales. In our case we will never go back to the Brass Rail."

Like a merry-go-round tangents can generate a centrifugal force that goes beyond their individual meanings.

Catapult Comments

Deliberation has its place, but every now and then, "swizzle-stick." Stir up the musty airs associated with the interviewing room. The analogy can be found in baseball and music. Compare a statistician reciting batting averages, hits, errors, RBIs, and win–loss percentages with radio announcer Russ Hodges screaming, "The Giants win the pennant! The Giants win the pennant! The Giants win the pennant!" (After Bobby Thomson hit a ninth inning, game-winning home run off Ralph Branca on October 3, 1951.)

Or match Beethoven's stirring "Ode to Joy" ending his Ninth Symphony to the following report on a concert by a time-methods specialist:

For considerable periods the oboe players had nothing to do. The numbers should be reduced, and the work spread out more evenly over the whole of the concert, thus eliminating peaks of activity.

It was noted that all twelve first violins were playing identical notes. This seems unnecessary duplication; the staff of that section should be drastically cut. If a large volume of sound is required, it could be obtained by means of electronic-amplifier apparatus.

Much effort was absorbed in the playing of sixteenth and so-called "Grace-notes." This is an excessive refinement. It is recommended that all notes should be rounded up to the nearest eighth-note. If this were done, it would be possible to use trainee and lower-grade operatives more exclusively.

There is too much repetition of some musical passages. Scores should be drastically pruned. No useful purpose is served by repeating on horns and wood-winds a passage which has already been adequately handled by the strings. It is also estimated that if all redundant passages were eliminated, the whole concert time would be reduced to twenty minutes, and there would be no need for an interval or intermission.

The conductor concurs generally with these recommendations, but expresses the opinion that there might be some falling-off in box-office receipts. In that unlikely event, it should be possible to close sections of the auditorium entirely, with a consequent savings in overhead, lighting, janitor service, heating, etc. [Author Unknown]

This straitjacket approach to music graphically underscores my central point: *You can be thorough and rational, but without verve, fail.* Spontaneity is a heartbeat, the systole and diastole of interviewing.

I admit that some of us are slower afoot than others, but all move faster toward objects of interest. *How can you catapult yourself into contention?*

1. Direct the conversation toward topics about which you have knowledge and passion. (My teenager sounds enfeebled when conversing about school, but get him on tennis and his voice skyrockets two octaves.)

2. At times use a rat-a-tat delivery conveying a plethora of ideas.

3. On occasion, surprise. Haydn did it by inserting a loud chord in his Symphony No. 94 (commonly called the "Surprise Symphony") to wake a drowsy audience. You can introduce a picture, chart, or drawing. Relate what you're saying to an artifact in the room. Raise your voice, stand up. Short of a backflip, do anything different to break the verbal monotony.

4. Sail with the current. Keep yourself up-to-date and informed on current affairs. Stay in fashion, so you'll have something to say. Read. Some suggestions:

   • The "Book Review" and "Week in Review" sections of your Sunday newspaper

- Alvin Toffler's *Future Shock* or *The Third Wave*—on understanding change and conflict in society
- Tom Peters's *Thriving on Chaos* or *In Search of Excellence* (with Robert H. Waterman, Jr.), about organizations and management
- John Naisbitt's *Megatrends* or *Megatrends 2000*, predicting future directions
- A quick read on the focal topic of this chapter is Max De Pree's *Leadership Is an Art.*
- *The One-Minute Manager®* by Ken Blanchard— three core principles of managing
- *Iacocca* by Lee Iacocca
- For humorous ideas:

    Dave Barry Turns 40 or *Dave Barry Talks Back*

    Robert Townsend's *Up the Organization*

    Arthur Bloch's *Murphy's Law*

    Erma Bombeck's *When You Look Like Your Passport Photo, It's Time to Go Home*

- *Conceptual Blockbusting* by James L. Adams, on thinking creatively
- *Please Understand Me* (David Keirsey and Marilyn Bates). Based on the concepts of Carl Jung and the "Myers-Briggs Type Indicators." You can complete the test and get a reading on your temperament.
- For musings about the human condition: Robert Fulghum's *All I Really Need to Know I Learned in Kindergarten* or *Uh-Oh*

- For contemporary issues like feminism and the changing role of males, see *Fire in the Belly* (Sam Keen) and *You Just Don't Understand* (Deborah Tannen).
- You should know the leading writings in your field, i.e., sales, finance, manufacturing, engineering, management, retailing, customer service, computers, government, office administration, and the like.

You may be asked what you have read recently. Come prepared.

.   .   .

Know what you're talking about,
but nobody likes a smart-ass.

.   .   .

Aspire to Greater Things

Even if you don't. Organizations want promotables at all levels—sales rep, secretary, hourly worker, truck operator, computer programmer, etc. To appear upward bound, display:

- A desire to learn new things
- An obsession with quality
- A sense of urgency
- A yen for long hours
- Goals

Let me emphasize goals (I briefly mentioned them on page 56). They are aspirations, a prediction about your future. Usually they're stated as results, an end state. A healthy exercise is periodically to write out goals for yourself. Why?

- To clarify where you're headed
- To make it easier to decide how to get there
- To shed some perspective on your present state
- To lay a foundation for self-improvement

On the next page jot down professional and personal goals. Divide them into short-term (to be accomplished in the next year) and long-term (two, five, ten years). Then circle the priority ones, those you definitely want to achieve. Your time should be built around them.

To help in this process I recommend *How to Get Control of Your Time and Your Life* by Alan Lakein, the best book I know on the subject.

Goals will become a topic of discussion in the interview. Know where you're going, at least for the moment.

Go Gung ho

The rallying cry of Carlson's Marine Raiders in World War II, "gung ho" has come to mean "damn the torpedoes, full speed ahead." Literally the Chinese word *kung-ho* denotes working together. Interviewers value both meanings.

Demonstrate impatience with inertia and mediocrity. Give examples of proaction, situations in which you took charge. Exhibit what Martin Luther King, Jr., called the "drum-major instinct."

Goals for Myself

Date_____

Professional	**Personal**
I. Short-term (within 12 months): E.g., learn to use WordPerfect, visit the assembly plant.	E.g., start piano lessons, take a trip to California.
II. Long-term (beyond 1 year): E.g., be promoted to supervisor, get an MBA.	E.g., spend a year in Europe, learn photography.

.   .   .

Your karma: "Do it now!"

.   .   .

This chapter has been about quasars, quintessence, and quantum theory. Quasars are celestial objects that give off enormous *energy* in outer outer space.

Quintessence is a fifth essence, next to air, fire, water, and earth. For our purposes it's *floy floy.*

In quantum theory *energy* is absorbed or radiated in intermittent fixed units. Scientists have calculated that by the age of sixty our eyes have been exposed to more light energy than would be unleashed by a nuclear blast. Take a few quantum leaps in the interview, emitting some of your spirit and liveliness.

What if you're a Caspar Milquetoast, Winnie the Pooh, Charlie Brown, or Walter Mitty? How do you radioactivate then?

True, everyone doesn't have Cyrano de Bergerac's panache. Everyone doesn't have a contagious personality, an uplifting style like JFK's, like General Schwarzkopf's. But, starting from some of the suggestions in this chapter, you can generate bursts of command, of ebullience, of charisma. You must, to distinguish yourself from the competition.

The benediction of Obi-Wan Kenobi, the *Star Wars* guru, provides an appropriate twist to hotshot floogie:

"The force be with you."

TIPS

- Bone up and perk up.
- Generate the same level of enthusiasm for interviewing as you do for your favorite pastime.
- Overconfidence beats shyness every time.
- Be flamboyant but don't "flaunt your daunt."
- Don't be a nodder.
- Don't whiffle-waffle.
- Convey you are a risk-taker but not a reckless driver.
- Be a VEP (Very Energetic Person).

Principle 8. Take the High Ground

• • •

A turning point in the Civil War was the Battle of Gettysburg, July 1863, when the 20th Regiment of Maine held Little Round Top against an overwhelming number of Confederate soldiers. In war and in growing-up fights a cardinal rule is: Control the high ground. From that vantage you get perspective, you can see what's going on, and your opponent has the handicap of fighting uphill.

So too with interviewing. Amid the tension and stresses of being evaluated, you must take charge. By control I mean:

- Managing time allotted
- Using the interview effectively
- Maintaining an even keel
- Accomplishing planned objectives in presenting yourself

The skill of the interviewer is not a variable. Nor are time, the quality of questions asked, or other applicants. No matter how brief an interview, how inept the interrogator, how shallow the questions, the responsibility for selling is yours. No excuses. You must, if necessary, turn the worst klutz into an effective interviewer.

To accomplish that let's look at:

- Interviewer Types
- Job Stereotypes
- Eight Control Techniques

Interviewer Types

Interviewers tend to exhibit behaviors that indicate their leanings, their basic approach to testing candidates. I submit ten types, (I confess, tongue-in-cheek), though in your job search I believe you will see the markings of many of them.

1. Dr. Frankenstein

As in the classic horror story, he creates monsters—monsters who are angry, rude, in poor disposition. He makes you uncomfortable.

Your Strategy: Hang tough. Induce a smile. That's your primary aim. Until you accomplish that, forget trying to sell yourself.

2. The Distractor

Distractors fidget, accept phone calls, look out the window, page through papers. They are uninvolved and inattentive.

Your Strategy: Change your physical position, vary your voice or stop talking. Let them fill the silence.

3. The Clam

Being interviewed by a Clam is like talking to a tree. Clams are mute and offer little information. You can't read them.

Your Strategy: Ask questions. What are you looking for in this position? What are the long-term objectives of the organization? What has been the greatest change in the business since you started working here?

4. The Peacock

Peacocks stroke their feathers and strut their importance. They play king and queen.

Your Strategy: Cater to their egos. Compliment them. Ask for advice.

5. The Huggermugger

Interviewers who act friendly, agree and nod yes, but behind the facade seek to rob you of that job. The ones most likely to say, "Don't call us, we'll call you."

Your Strategy: Be wary, but barge ahead. When you suspect a trap, change the subject. At the close ask them to declare interest one way or the other.

6. The Inquisitor

Fires questions like a Gatling gun.

Your Strategy: Take a deep breath, deliberate, tamp your pipe, ask for a drink of water or use some other stall. Bide your time.

7. The Clock-Watcher

Time binders, they adjust their watches, act as if they should be somewhere else and usually start the interview with, "I'm running a tight schedule."

Your Strategy: Don't rush. Zero in on priority points, then try to be interesting enough so they forget time and schedule.

8. Dr. Know-It-All

Has all the answers, an expert on everything.
Your Strategy: Go along. Avoid arguments or debates. Stay focused on your message.

9. Doubting Thomas

Suspects all applicants of lying and exaggerating their experience and capabilities.
Your Strategy: Give plenty of examples. Suggest Tom contact your references for further information.

10. The Company Man

Proud to be a part of the organization. Has only good to say about it. Uses the third-person-plural pronoun "we."
Your Strategy: Talk about loyalty, the value of teamwork, and your history cooperating with others on projects.

Of course, these are not discrete categories. Interviewers slide from one to another based on the kind of day they're having and on your performance. What about Mr. Nice Guy or the Expert Interviewer? Don't worry, they'll stand out like two nuns in a singles' bar. They make your task easy, giving you ample chance to display your wares.

Job Stereotypes

Departments and positions develop character (and characters!). You might call it stereotyping, more false than true, but understanding the patterns can be useful in controlling the interview. If your interviewer falls into one of these categories, what is the appropriate approach?

SALES

Deal in the present	Short-term oriented
Work and play hard	Aggressive, impulsive
Personality oriented	Big spenders
Act now, think later	Always on the run
Rugged competitors	Practical

Your Strategy: Demonstrate floy floy. Play up the significance of qualifying customers and getting close to them, grubbing for new accounts and achieving quotas. Return to your karma: Do it now.

MARKETING

Long-range planners	Intellectual
Media oriented	Analytical
Controlled	Superior
Theorists	Isolated
Focus-group oriented	

Your Strategy: Underline the importance of marketing research, analyzing data and thoroughness. Cite products and advertising campaigns that you think are especially effective. Emphasize analysis first, and action second.

INFORMATION SYSTEMS

Paper producers	An odd lot
Detached	Talk computerese
Rigid	The mystery department

They make others conform to their schedule.

Your Strategy: Stress data processing–user cooperation and the need for educating users on the capability of computers.

Discuss the future of computers in the operation of organizations. Talk technical.

MANUFACTURING

Hard workers	Not systems oriented
Inflexible	Hard hats
Uneducated	Unpolished
Not cost conscious	Grunts

Your Strategy: Meeting production standards—that's what it's all about. Nuts and bolts, hard hitting, hard work. Highlight safety matters. Review ways to improve quality. Keep it practical.

ENGINEERING

Procrastinators	Negative attitude
Academic	Ivory tower thinkers
Indecisive	Unreceptive to ideas
Deal in black and white terms	Humorless
Won't get their hands dirty	

Your Strategy: Voice a preference for systems. Don't move to point B until you've covered all aspects of A. Use mechanical and electrical examples. Talk technical.

FINANCE

Bean counters	Picky, detailed
Bureaucrats	Tunnel vision
"Analysis by paralysis"	Boring
Conservative	Formal, stiff

Your Strategy: Watch your p's and q's and decimal points. Headline sound budgeting and airtight controls. Be attentive to detail and know your numbers.

PERSONNEL/EMPLOYEE RELATIONS

Slow to act	Political
Monday morning quarterbacks	Paper shufflers
Soft-soapers	Inconsistent
Policy policemen	Run scared

Your Strategy: Human relations are all. Tend to people and the rest will take care of itself. Show interest in compensation and benefits planning, performance appraisals, employee handbooks and career pathing. Your key skills are interpersonal relations, communicating and negotiating.

MAINTENANCE

Unreliable	Operate as an island
Resist change	Old school
Sloppy	"Mr. Goodwrench"

First reaction is, "It can't be done"

Your Strategy: Prevention is the watchword. If employees took care of facilities and equipment on a daily basis, there would be fewer mechanical emergencies. Focus on troubleshooting skills and technical knowledge.

UNION

Hard-nosed	Complainers
Avoid problems	Slow up production
Lack of initiative	Don't care

Make mountains out of molehills
Only concerned with pay and benefits
Can't see the bigger picture
Want responsibility without accountability

Your Strategy: Stand ready to address three ways managers screw up and make life difficult for employees. Also three ways to raise morale. Talk like the rank and file.

MANAGEMENT

Demanding	Unresponsive
Jump to conclusions	Blame throwers
Hardheaded	Must have the last word
Take the credit	Distant
Don't follow through	Play favorites
Never admit they are wrong	

Don't recognize employees for their good works

Your Strategy: Top-flight managers take the high ground. Suggest ways to increase productivity and motivate people. Stand for hands-on management, employee involvement and risk-taking. Relate everything to "the bottom line."

Your interviewer may not conform to any of these profiles, but knowing that different functions tend to develop different likes and preferences can be important to sensing control. People act on stereotypes, no matter how untrue and unjust.

Eight Control Techniques

1. Scope Interviewers.

Read their clues (e.g., interested in people, numbers, deadlines?), take into account job differences and adapt your approach accordingly. Look for a smile of agreement, a grimace or frown of disapproval or a questioning look, and respond to it. Keep eye contact.

2. Encourage Interviewers to Talk.

The more they expound the more you'll know what's important to them, and the less time they'll have to put you in cul-de-sac situations.

3. Be Unflappable in Crisis.

You may be kept waiting, the interviewer might throw you a curve, or you could find yourself surprised with more than one examiner present. Some deliberately move the goalposts to see how you react. Don't whip-stall. Remember you can handle two or three tasks at once, and you don't mind deadlines or last minute scheduling changes.

If your stomach does a half-gainer, your heart pole-vaults to your throat and you can barely talk for cottonmouth, windhover like a hawk until you resight the target. To reinforce your unflappability, give examples of crises you have faced and onerous tasks you have performed nobly.

4. Take Advantage of Difficult Questions.

They present opportunities to shine. Follow this formula:

A = R + E
Answer = Response + Example

Support every response with examples and anecdotes from your experience. Interviewers want specifics, concrete explanations. If you get stuck, then, as suggested earlier, divert the question or answer a related one.

Here are two samples of ways interviewers try to test you:

Sample A: "Sell me this pen [or some other object in the office]."
Guidelines for responding:

a. Establish need—why the interviewer should have a pen.

b. State features of the pen—smooth line, clip-on, non-smudge ink, etc.

c. List benefits to the interviewer—neat copy, dependable performance, etc.

d. Ask for the interviewer's reaction and handle objections.

e. Close the sale.

Sample B: "How would you handle this situation . . . [a problem from the work setting]?"
Guidelines for responding:

a. Define the problem by asking questions.

b. Identify two or three causes.

c. Suggest two or three possible solutions.

d. Recommend one to try—it isn't final until you test it. This gives you an out if the interviewer finds fault.

e. Adapt or change your approach to the problem, based on the results.

An example of problem-solving appears on pages 96–97.

5. Take Stock of Your Progress.

Halfway through, mentally tabulate the positive and negative reactions of the interviewer. If too many negatives, change course. Listen to your instincts for telltale signs of teetering. Trust your belly button. If you're bored, so is the interviewer. If you're uncomfortable, so is the interviewer.

·   ·   ·

If you don't feel things are going well, they're not.

·   ·   ·

6. Set the Pace.

You need to tugboat interviewers toward your objectives. Just a gentle push. When things get too hectic, deliberate; when too slow, accelerate. Like the Indianapolis 500, jockey for pole position. Perhaps a better analogy is a symphony in four movements.

Adagio—Start carefully, feeling your way.

Andante—Increase the tempo. You're loosening up.

Scherzo—The turning point of the interview. Pick up and pep up. Introduce some fun.

Allegro molto—A fast finish, leaving the interviewer breathless and impressed.

Your objective is to stay in sync and not "catch a crab." That's what happens in sculling when one member of an eight-oared shell breaks the rhythm—you get an oar in the gut!

"Is this interview going to last much longer? Isn't it time for lunch?"

7. Ask Intelligent Questions.

Aristotle wrote, "To know what to ask is already to know half." You will be judged on the quality of your questions, and the quality of your questions will help you stay on track.

Questions not to ask (unless you're a shoo-in):

- When will I be promoted?
- How big an office will I get?
- Will I have a parking space?

- How many sick days do you provide?
- Does your health insurance cover dog grooming?
- How long for lunch?
- How many days' vacation?
- Will you relocate my horse (or two-ton rock garden)?
- What time do I have to be at work in the morning?
- Do you provide coffee?
- What holidays do you give off?
- I'm in need of a little money right now. Do you make loans?

Employers interpret these as your interest in what you will take from the organization rather than what you will contribute.

Questions to clarify:

- I'm not sure I understand.
- Could you rephrase that question?
- Can you give me an example?
- Could you say more on that?

Questions for information (see also "Cross-Question," page 208):

- What are the major responsibilities of the position?
- What are plans for the organization over the next five years?
- What's the chief capability you're looking for in this position?
- Would it be possible for me to tour the facilities? Travel with one of your sales reps?

Most applicants ask more questions in purchasing stereo speakers than they do in choosing employment. Interviewers dress up job descriptions to make them more attractive. You must probe underneath the dressing.

.   .   .

It is better to know some of the questions
than all the answers.
—James Thurber

.   .   .

8. Avoid Desperation.

Those in control don't panic and don't get defensive. No matter how long you've been beating the pavement, restraint is required. Be patient. Good things happen to good people—who know what they're doing.

A word on compensation and benefits is appropriate here. What you'll settle for is directly related to how much you need the job, or want it.

My advice:

- Get the employer to state salary range.
- Don't give your current salary unless specifically asked.
- If asked, inflate your earnings to fit with the current offering.
- When stating salary demands, keep in mind research at the State University of New York at Buffalo. They concluded that applicants who have low salary expec-

tations generally are offered low salaries. The more money you ask for, the more you get.[25]

- Don't haggle over money and benefits until you're the preferred candidate.

Seize the high ground. David outclassed Goliath by exploiting his own strength: accuracy with a sling; and his greatest limitation: size. Goliath underestimated and left himself open for a lethal blow. Interviewers assume the proportions of Goliath. Take advantage of your underdog role. Maneuver them, all the time ensuring they feel at the helm.

---

[25]Obviously, there's a limit. You don't demand $50,000 if you're applying for a short-order cook or checkout clerk. If a range is indicated, stay within that range.

You can achieve control by:

- *Reacting* to content and mannerisms of interviewers.
- *Sticking to what you do best*, staying within your limits. (Heed the Buddhist adage: "One should not add legs to a snake.")
- *Understanding the inner workings and nuances of interviewing* better than the person sitting across from you.

Developing power to direct the interview is like painting a portrait. You have the brush. Only you know what the final canvas should look like.

TIPS

- Lead the interviewer into your comfort zone.
- Manage time by discussing priority points first.
- Assess your progress at least once during the interview, and vary your approach accordingly.
- Go into your best Socratic crouch and ask at least six questions.
- It is better to respond to the wrong question than look like a dimwit answering the one posed.
- Keep your cool.
- Endplay interviewers so all the pieces left show strength and no weakness.
- Control goes to the one who understands the dynamics of interviewing.

Principle 9. Exit as an Associate: Making the Interviewer Feel Good

· · ·

We began a strategy for excelling in interviews with your entrance as an alien. If you pull off the principles in this book you will leave an associate. I choose the word carefully. You cannot become a colleague or friend, and that's not the objective. Your task is to connect, to bring into being a relationship. Hopefully interviewers will see you as someone with whom they would want to work.

How to accomplish that? Divide it into two parts:

- Making Interviewers Feel Good
- Leaving Lasting Impressions

Making Interviewers Feel Good

This strategy stems from Myth #11 (Part One). In any struggle between facts and feelings, bet on feelings every time. Fernando Henrique Cardoso, Brazil's professor-politician, found that out the hard way. In his first run for office in 1985, he was campaigning for mayor of São Paulo against a "people's candidate." Contemplating victory, he had his picture taken sitting in the mayor's chair, a photograph that somehow appeared on the front page of a São Paulo newspaper the morning of the election. The worst happened, as it has a tendency to do. He lost. Reflecting on that deflating day, he concluded, "I was trained in a world [academia] where 'brilliance' comes from reason and not passion."

You, as do politicians, obtain jobs through passion.

.   .   .

> Your charge is not to get the job;
> it's to make the interviewer feel good.

.   .   .

This is a major theme. Miss that and you miss the job. Leave the interviewer smiling, and the rest will follow as night the day (as the poet would say).

What's the basis for Principle 9? Observation. Look around you. In human relationships rationality is a myth foisted on

us by the ancient Greeks.[26] They believed everything could
be reduced to syllogisms. You know:

All apples are fruit;
Fruit is edible;
Therefore all apples are edible.

Sounds good, but 'tain't necessarily so. Some apples are green,
some rotten (and in lore some may be poisoned by the evil
witch or a serpent).

Pick up any newspaper and see how many examples of
reasonableness you find in the world. In all wars ever fought,
both sides claimed God and logic on their side. Few family
disputes are solved by rationality. Boss-employee relations
have more to do with emotions than job responsibilities—
performance appraisals attest to that.

In Yiddish there's a delightful explanation of this phenomenon:

"Mein pupik zucked mir azoy."
("My belly button tells me it's so.")

Recall the admonition in Principle 8: "Trust your belly button." I suspect much of human affairs is run by the Belly
Button Method (BBM). We decide first, then build a logical
explanation. It may be an important myth to preserve, that
we are sensible in our dealings with each other, but the BBM
prevails in interviewing.

Given that, how do you avoid being disliked, and what can
you do to help interviewers feel good?

Ways to Turn Off Interviewers (taken from actual cases)

- Bring your mother to the interview.
- Wear a toupee.

[26]The British philosopher Bertrand Russell mused, "Aristotle calls man the
rational animal. All my life I have been seeking evidence to confirm this."

- Come with a snake around your neck and indicate your pet goes everywhere with you.
- Tote a gun that shows when you unbutton your jacket.
- Wear fifteen pounds of jewelry.
- Tap-dance across the room.
- Hide behind your hair.
- Balance your checkbook during the interview.
- Apply makeup in front of interviewers.
- Threaten them: "My grandma will put a curse on you if you don't hire me."
- Comment that "they just don't understand our generation." ("They" being the interviewer's generation.)
- Insist "That was okay in your day, but now things are different."
- Contradict interviewers: "You're wrong there. No way will robots take the place of workers."
- Bring out a line of cosmetics and launch into your sales pitch.
- Wear dark glasses so all they see is their reflection.
- Show up in your jogging suit.
- Talk about your bed-wetting days.
- Ask to use the interviewer's telephone, and call your psychiatrist to discuss an answer to a question.
- If the interviewer takes a phone call, pull out your fried-chicken lunch and eat it on her desk.
- When the interview gets sticky, leave the room to meditate.
- Challenge the interviewer to arm-wrestle.

- Or more gentlemanly, bring your little pinball game with you and double-dare the interviewer to a winner-take-all contest.

Yes, believe it or not, all true.

Ways to Turn on Interviewers

Fluff Their Pillows.

Recognize interviewer brainwork. Compliment them. You can do that without being a sycophant, fawning all over the place. I don't even imply chumminess. I mean look for good in their actions, and don't hesitate to comment, "I like that, I never quite thought of it that way." Hitchhike on their ideas: "Yes, if I can build on that . . ." or "That reminds me of . . ." or "I agree, and if I can take that one step further . . ." A little recognition goes a long way in reinforcing others' belief in themselves.

Be a Relevance-Raiser.

An RR is somebody who on the run and with a glance can size up a situation, find something of value to others and make that the first order of business. In his seemingly unwitting way New York Yankee outfielder Yogi Berra expressed a talent of Relevance Raisers in one of his famous Yogi-isms: "You can observe a lot just by watching."

In Principle 2 I wrote about jump-starting interviewers by riveting in on information close to them—hobbies, a book on the shelf, something about the building or location or personnel.

You and the interviewer operate in different worlds, and little understanding occurs unless you develop a base for it. *Communication* is derived from the Latin *communis*, meaning "common."

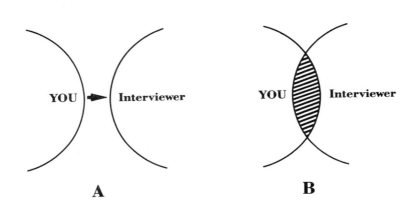

Diagram A represents the gap as you walk in the door. Just answering questions is not necessarily communicating. It's one way.

Diagram B models what you must do throughout the interview: Find common ground from which to send and receive messages. Relating, finding where your two worlds overlap, can be the difference between passing and failing.

Get interviewers to talk by asking about their jobs, their experiences with the organization and in the community. Present information that would be useful or strike a familiar chord, e.g., "I was surprised to find that your founder came from a town near where I grew up."

For other ideas on relevance-raising refer to the strategies for Interviewer Types and Job Stereotypes in Principle 8. WARNING: Take care not to act superior or embarrass interviewers, trying to impress them with your knowledge.

"You seem to fit in here, Henderson. I think we have a job for you."

Be Congruent.

You must appear to fit with the interviewer, the job and the organization. Reinforce interviewer values, many of them itemized in Principle 3. The major ones are:

- A taste for hard work
- A nose for success
- An eye on profit
- A feel for people

Act as a Buoy.

You must put the interviewer at ease, break the monotony and beam in the frequently deadly conditions of an employment inquest. Anxiety is a necessary but disagreeable part of the process. One way to overcome butterflies is cheer. I don't mean making whoopee or singing hosannas. Instead, approach interviewers with bounce, with chirpiness. It's contagious. It'll reflect in their mannerisms. Talk to them as if they were a friendly neighbor.

Pick someone who makes you smile, who makes you feel good. What does this person do to cause those feelings? Then adapt and practice techniques to fit you.

Buoyancy will keep your chances afloat.

.   .   .

> If the interviewer is more cheerful at the end of the interview than at the beginning, you will move on to the next step in the employment process.

.   .   .

Use Your Sense of Humor.

Everyone has one; some exercise it more than others. Some-where in the interview "a laugh, a laugh, your career for a laugh." Chuckle at yourself. Build merriment from context. One anxious applicant pointed to a NO SMOKING sign in the waiting room and kidded, "How about if we compromise— I'll inhale only."

In Principle 2 I recommended against telling jokes, and I repeat it here. Unless your timing is impeccable your chestnuts will fall on soggy ground.

"Have you heard the one about the seven Polacks . . ."

Lose Yourself.

Throughout, the Bible echoes one theme: He who loses himself gains the world. That mini-sermon applies here. You must unknot your feelings and concerns, and overcome normal fear of interviewing. Try setting this as your aim: *How do I make the person across from me an effective interviewer?* Your behavior will be quite different than if you start with: How do I get through this third degree?

In botany heliotropism is the tendency of plants to turn toward the sun. Grow sun skills to attract, to draw interviewers toward you. One criterion of success is: *Did time pass quickly? Did one hour seem like twenty minutes?* If so, it's likely you and the interviewer connected.

Leaving Lasting Impressions

A surgeon friend tells me his guiding principle is *"Close good!* No matter what else, sew 'em up with style." How do you "close good," stitching an unforgettable embroidery?

> Cross-Question
> Leave Some Thing of Value
> Outline Your Position
> Seek Commitment to Next Steps
> Execute a Follow-through Plan.

Cross-Question.

As the interview winds down, go back over the discourse and fill in missing information about the job and the organization by asking questions.

- Could you describe a typical day for someone in this position?
- With whom would I be working?
- What decisions does this person have authority to make?
- How much interaction is there with other departments?
- What is the history for advancement in this division?
- Is this a new position?
- What's the biggest change in the business since you started?
- If you had to state one quality, and only one, for the person in this job, what would it be?
- Could you show me how this division is organized?

Ask questions about the business, using the vocabulary of the organization and industry, terminology *you* picked up during the conversation. Keep in mind that *you* are interviewing *them*. Before you step out of that room, you need to determine if this is the right job for you.

Leave Some Thing of Value.

By now you should know the key job requirements. Highlight one strength, a uniqueness that qualifies you and only you. If the job is a creative one, emphasize your ability to invent alternatives; if mundane, underscore your attention to detail.

Create a halo effect, one outstanding trait or accomplishment that the interviewer will generalize to other endeavors no matter how unrelated. If you scored the winning touchdown in the last minute of a championship game, that will do. Or you sold more unscented deodorant than anybody in the history of the company. Or you graduated in the top 10 percent of your class.

What do you want the interviewer to remember? Don't dilute your finale by listing four or five attributes. One or, at best, two virtues are about all interviewers can handle.

"In summary, I'm trustworthy, loyal, helpful, friendly, courteous, kind, obedient, cheerful, thrifty, brave, clean, reverent . . ."

Leave some *thing* the interviewer can touch, hold, refer to—a written paper, diagram, project, model. All interviewers suffer from a mild form of Alzheimer's, especially in multiple sessions like college screening. I've seen their mnemonic notes:

- "Scar above right cheek."
- "Big nose with mustache."

- "Balding with dark-rimmed glasses."
- "Dark penetrating eyes."
- "The one who drove up in a Ferrari."
- "The tall thin one."

To counter lapses of memory, leave a tangible remembrance.

Outline Your Position.

Come out of the closet. Let interviewers know where you stand.

On the interview: "I can't be sure I'll get the job, but I appreciate the time and enjoyed this session."

On the position: "I like what I see. I'm very interested. The requirements seem to fit my goals and capabilities."

.   .   .

Never ride in the interviewer's blind spot.

.   .   .

But "*Siempre la trampa*," the Spanish warn: "Keep an ace in the hole." For instance, "I have three more interviews and there's one job I'm seriously considering." Period. Interviewers will speculate about the rest. They'll react, giving you clues to their resolve.

Seek Commitment to Next Steps.

Don't leave without agreement on what follows. You need to know your standing and whether you should pursue further. Unless all applicants have been seen or you are an obvious standout, interviewers will not commit themselves. Here are some signs of their receptiveness:

Encouraging	*Hopeless*
Your BBR is high.	Your BBR is low.
"Could you stay for lunch?"	The interview is cut short.
A date is set for you to come back.	They refuse to commit to anything.
Enthusiastic reaction.	A low-key good-bye.
"I would like you to meet the vice president."	"I have many more people to interview. . . ."
"Call before you accept another offer."	"Don't call us . . ."

Ask directly, "How do you think I fit what you're looking for?" If they say, "We'll let you know," ask, "When?" If interviewers go into a song and dance, move on. Better to find out now than waste worry time afterward.

Execute a Follow-through Plan.

Follow-through is "hanging in there," that lasting quality all top salespeople possess. It requires record-keeping to prevent memory lapses and ensure attention to detail. Frequently that makes the difference in job-getting. It's the shortstop's extra two steps, the boss's compliment, flowers to a friend, a soldier's clean rifle, remembering a name, that separates winners from losers and sometimes the living from the dead. Selling yourself depends on the little things.

What does follow-through consist of?

1. Immediately after the interview make notes for future action:
   - Names of secretaries and other employees you met
   - Likes and dislikes of the interviewer
   - Personal information about the interviewer, e.g., family, hobbies, interests, projects
   - Personal information about the secretary or receptionist
   - Data on the organization
   - Who are the decision-makers?
   - Any unusual occurrences
   - Directions on how to get there. If you're invited back, you don't have to ask again.
   - Next steps and deadlines

2. Within one week write the interviewer a one-pager. Include:
   - An I-like-what-I-saw message
   - A personal note that will help him or her recall the interview
   - Anything left out, e.g., "You asked about my performance under stress. I should have mentioned my experience at MPI . . ."
   - A strong statement about why you qualify
   - A comment about some interviewer activity—"I hope your speech at the personnel conference went well."

- "I look forward to hearing from you in two weeks."
  (Or whatever deadline was set)

This letter brings your name in front of the interviewer again, reiterates your enthusiasm for the job, and demonstrates that you can write coherently.

3. Telephone to thank the interviewer and/or secretary for their hospitality.

4. Ask a third party of influence or somebody the interviewer knows to call or write a backup letter. If you don't hear by the agreed-upon deadline, call. Not anxiously, but informing the company that you're nearing decision time and would like to know its plans.

There are no trade secrets to following through. It's a matter of persistence, tracking, and doing—doing what you say you're going to do. It's being a finisher.

We all collect things. My weakness is wine bottles (before and after they're empty). Somehow they seem more substantial than most objects. One reason is the kick, that indentation at the bottom, which adds strength and makes it appear you're drinking more than the bottle actually contains. You need a kick of sorts. At the close you must stand tall and appear attractive and substantial.

Employ the Doppler effect in which sound seems to rise in pitch from an approaching object and drop in pitch when its source recedes, like a train whistle. You should be coming on at the close. End your dramatic aria with a high "C."

Leave not footprints in sand that will be wiped out by the next applicant to come along. With the authority of a confident candidate, gently stamp your imprint on the forehead of the interviewer.

TIPS

- Increase the interviewer's self-esteem.
- Turn on interviewers to laugh, to enjoy.
- Underline and repeat why you are uniquely qualified for the job.
- "Don't squander your clout." Save something for the finish.
- Avoid dickering at the end (e.g., salary, starting date), lest you find yourself "in the thick of thin things."
- Set forth your modus operandi as: "How would I do the job if I owned the company?"
- Listen to your BBR, your internal rhythms. They know.
- Cross-question.
  Leave some thing of value.
  Outline your position.
  Seek commitment to next steps.
  Execute a follow-through plan.

Part Three

. . .

PUTTING IT ALL TOGETHER

. . .

Part One detailed the state of interviewing and myths involved.

Part Two spelled out nine principles for passing your big test.

Part Three traces the translation of principles into action. It answers such questions as:

- How do you implement ideas in this book?
- What does Rumpelstiltskin have to do with interviewing?
- What are the key elements of learning and self-development?
- How do you evaluate your performance?
- What are the next steps?
- If you fall on your face, then what?

- What are the four T's for taking charge of your career path?
- What are the ten commandments of interviewing?
- What does a successful interview look like?

PUTTING IT ALL TOGETHER

· · ·

We do not what we ought;
What we ought not, we do;
And lean upon the thought
That chance will bring us through.
—Matthew Arnold, "Empedocles on Etna"

On Montgomery's defeat of Rommel in Egypt in 1942, Winston Churchill declared, "Now this is not the end. It is not even the beginning of the end. But it is perhaps the end of the beginning."

I would characterize this book as the end of the beginning, a preface. In *The Strawberry Statement* James Simon Kunen, a Columbia University student, observes, "It's God-day today. Everybody makes the worship scene for an hour and comes out feeling good. That's the trouble. They should come out feeling like doing good, but instead they feel good already without doing anything." The work is yet undone.

This book is not a ready-made cake mix.

Most interviewers are ignorant of the factors that influence the way they gather data and make decisions. That doesn't mean you can feed them slumgullion and expect acceptance.

You must start from scratch with painstaking preparation and your own recipe.

Give them your best dish.

Opportunity is not coming—it's here. How do you get your money's worth out of this book? How do you transform principles into practice? Approach it from three perspectives:

- Learning and Self-Development
- A Strategy for Action
- Four T's to Keep in Mind

Learning and Self-Development

Learning is not going to school.

Learning is not reading a book.

Learning is not even passing a test.

Learning is the application of ideas to your daily life that results in a change of behavior, thought, emotion or well-being. Adult learning is deliberate and personal.

The model on the next page represents one explanation of how we gain knowledge and wisdom.

Adapt.

The sum total of our life experiences comprises our comprehensions and apprehensions. Over the years we induce ways of doing, thinking, feeling, from direct experience and observing others. The broader our adventures the greater the chance for development. We adapt learnings to fit our capabilities and comfort zone.

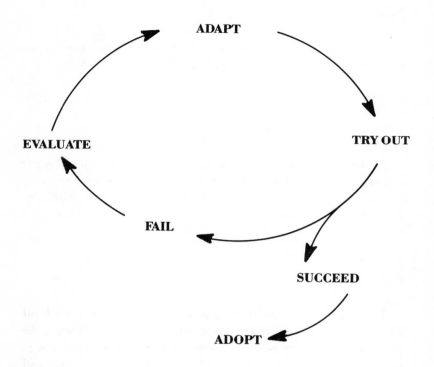

Try Out.

We discover if things we see, hear, touch, will work for us by trying them out. An untested idea is subject to error and fallacy. T. H. Huxley once said of the English philosopher Herbert Spencer, "Oh! you know, Spencer's idea of a tragedy is a deduction killed by a fact."

Succeed.

Three cheers. Celebrate. Success breeds confidence. (Success also breeds complacency. Guard against that.)

Adopt.

Embrace your triumphs, even if those around doubt your efforts. Mark Twain said it wryly: "What sustains me may kill you." Don't mess with your strengths. If they work for you, stay with them.

Fail.

Ah, there's the rub, that nasty four-letter word we have been conditioned to fear and cover up. In school we were penalized for every wrong answer, so we learned early not to step forward unless we were right, which translated into "have the teacher's answer." Look around you. I suspect the most successful people have suffered the most failures, were able to step back from the pain of not succeeding and derive lessons for future action.[27]

---

[27]Abraham Lincoln suffered ten election losses on his way to the presidency. Winston Churchill failed English academies. High school administrators recommended that Thomas Edison's parents withdraw him from classes because he would never make it. (That was probably the greatest piece of counseling in the history of education!)

.   .   .

Error is the soil of learning.

.   .   .

Evaluate.

When your efforts detour, find out why. What can you learn to prevent future disasters? Was it something you did? The action of others? Or some snafu in the situation itself? Ask for colleagues' assessments. They bring perspective to your own judgments.

Adapt.

We have come full circle. Learning spirals around, out from, and back to our line of experience. Perspective on our victories and defeats allows us to think and act in new ways, hopefully reducing apprehension and increasing comprehension.

I believe this is the way we develop: Adapt-Try Out-Succeed or Fail-Evaluate-Adapt, a circular process of growth relative to ongoing experiences. We tend to resist learning because we have no guide for action, no means for experimenting, for testing and retesting our potential and no support when we fail.

How does the model relate to improving your chances for employment?

A Strategy for Action

In the 1988 vice-presidential campaign Dan Quayle was criticized for being programmed by advisers. Frustrated, he announced, "Now it's my turn—[from here on] I'm my own handler!" And now it's your turn. Honcho your own career search.

The following four steps form a blueprint for upgrading your versatility in interviewing.

Step 1. Read and retrieve ideas and techniques from this book, your previous interviews and experiences of fellow searchers. Reading without reflection is a dead end.

On pages 226–227 jot down knowledge and skills:

- You feel comfortable with
- You want to learn

Then lay out how you plan to use them in your interviews.

Step 2. **Practice → record → assess → practice.**
Practice the techniques and skills you wrote in the last two columns on the following pages. Follow the guidelines for simulating on pages 62–63.

Record your trial runs. I strongly recommend videotaping so you can see mannerisms as well as words. Alice in Wonderland surmised, "How do I know what I think until I see what I have to say?"

Assess each videotaped practice, noting tone of voice and mannerisms that are disturbing. Use the evaluation form on the next two pages.

Practice some more. Try those methods that did not work well until you feel confident with them.

Step 3. Interview. In the Walt Disney movie *The Sword and the Stone,* Merlin the Wizard is trying to explain to a child which feathers a bird uses to take off and fly when an owl explains, "One learns to fly simply by flying." There is no substitute for the real thing. If you interview twenty times with no offers, don't declare bankruptcy. Count yourself lucky. As long as you learn from each one, you are twenty times smarter.

Step 4. Evaluate. Complete the twenty-seven-item questionnaire (pages 228–229) immediately after each interview. Immediately, because then your reactions will be fresh and accurate. The first page consists of fourteen scaled items, the second asks open-ended questions. This analysis will help you plan an improved approach to subsequent interviews.

Declaration of Commitment

Techniques/ Skills I Feel Confident Using	Techniques/ Skills I Want to Develop	How I Plan to Implement Them
Principle 1:		
Principle 2:		
Principle 3:		
Principle 4:		

Techniques/ Skills I Feel Confident Using	Techniques/ Skills I Want to Develop	How I Plan to Implement Them
Principle 5:		
Principle 6:		
Principle 7:		
Principle 8:		
Principle 9:		

Analyzing How I Did in the Interview

(Circle one number on each scale.)

1. How comfortable do I feel (BBR)?

   └─ · · · · ─┘
   1 2 3 4 5 6

2. How satisfied am I with my performance?

   └─ · · · · ─┘
   1 2 3 4 5 6

3. Did I prepare properly?

   └─ · · · · ─┘
   1 2 3 4 5 6

4. How interesting was the interview?

   └─ · · · · ─┘
   1 2 3 4 5 6

5. Did I make a positive impression in the first five minutes?

   └─ · · · · ─┘
   1 2 3 4 5 6

6. Did I convey stability?

   └─ · · · · ─┘
   1 2 3 4 5 6

7. Did I listen and ask questions?

   └─ · · · · ─┘
   1 2 ·3 4 5 6

8. Did I express myself clearly?

   └─ · · · · ─┘
   1 2 3 4 5 6

9. Was I enthusiastic?

   └─ · · · · ─┘
   1 2 3 4 5 6

10. Were there smiles and laughter?

   └─ · · · · ─┘
   1 2 3 4 5 6

11. Was I in control?

   └─ · · · · ─┘
   1 2 3 4 5 6

12. Did the interviewer like me?

   └─ · · · · ─┘
   1 2 3 4 5 6

13. Did the interviewer feel good?

   └─ · · · · ─┘
   1 2 3 4 5 6

14. To what degree do I fit the job and the organization?

   └─ · · · · ─┘
   1 2 3 4 5 6

15. What surprises occurred in the interview?

16. What did I do well?

17. What went poorly?

18. What would the interviewer say are my strengths?

19. My weaknesses?

20. What questions could I have answered better?

21. What questions should I have asked?

22. How was the pacing? Too slow? Too fast?

23. What points did I leave out?

24. Will they offer me the job?

25. Do I want it?

26. How will I follow up?

27. What techniques and skills do I need to work on?

Four T's to Keep in Mind

Interviewing is the defining moment in the hunt for employment. Some call it Crunch City. I call it Chance City, an opportunity to pull yourself out of job jitters and take charge of your destiny. Ezra Pound defined a slave as "one who waits for someone else to come and free him."

As you seek new career horizons, keep in mind four T's.

Thought

Touch

Technique

Timing

Thought is the "what," the knowledge part of interviewing. I have tried to describe it as a thinking-through process that requires planning, design and content.

Touch is the feeling component—establishing rapport, tuning in on the same wavelength as interviewers. Not chemistry, that's a nonentity. I hear managers declare, "The chemistry has to be right," as if some ethereal element determines outcomes. *What governs the outcome is behaving in specific ways to connect with interviewers.*

Touch*ing* is getting them to like you. Touch*ing* is "chemistry."

Technique is the "how," the implementation. It's possible to have great thoughts and feelings, but not convey them to interviewers. You must deliver, and *delivery requires a craft*. How to hone your craft has been the thrust of this book.

Timing is the "when." Thought, touch and technique are necessary, but timing is essential. Many correct decisions have fallen short because they were proposed at the wrong time. Watching TV sitcoms or reading the comics, note how much humor relies on phrasing and synchronization.

What are some timing issues in interviewing?

- Scheduling (see page 60)
- When to volunteer information

- When to stop talking and let the interviewer take over
- The uses of humor
- When to question
- Changing the subject
- Repetition
- When to ask about money matters

How do you develop crisp timing? By learning from episodes of bad timing, so you recognize the signs.

Throughout the book we have been exploring ways to improve Thought, Touch, Technique, and Timing in interviewing. Think of it as a triangulation process.

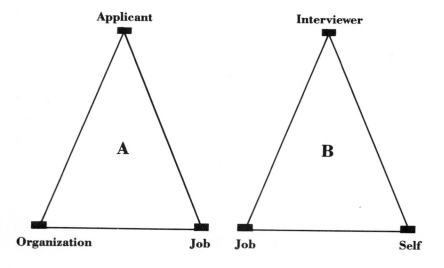

Applicant

A

Organization   **Job**

Interviewer

B

Job   **Self**

A represents what interviewers think is happening. They start from two points, the organization and the job, and believe if they perform the appropriate trigonometric operation, they'll locate a winner.

B depicts the actual state from your angle. Two known points exist—you and the desired job. Before and during the interview you estimate the relationship between the two, and from that, position yourself with the interviewer. This positioning, this interaction, is the determining factor in securing a job.

ONE LAST WORD TO
THE READER

. . .

The night before his inauguration in 1789 George Washington wrote a friend, "I approach this . . . with feelings not unlike those of a culprit who is going to his place of execution." Old George may have expressed your sentiments on interviewing.

Despite nervousness and uncertainty, don't crater out. Work at it until you can brag as one interviewee wrote poetically: "Armed with information and experience I arrested fear."

You, as we all do, carry your boundary to the employment search, but within that boundary is a vast unexplored potential. I have held many jobs, and admit unabashedly that *I never took a job for which I was qualified.* But I knew enough to pass the interview. If you possess the basic vocational requirements, you'll learn the job as you perform it. That is not the issue.

Your concern is getting there. Erving Goffman, the late University of Pennsylvania sociologist, devoted his study to the "management of impressions." He postulated that we are essentially performers whose main business is fabricating an identity. That's one way to look at development, and I see no inherent evil in such a view.

Effective interviewing is the management of impressions. No one can know you in forty minutes, or in forty hours for that matter. Therefore, style becomes substance.

Recommendations in this book are based on practice, not theory. Success is in the orchestration of many techniques and approaches. You are the composer. Combine elements to produce your sound—music no one can duplicate because it is your unique melody. Tone it well.

So heads up. Do all you can with what you have—and it's much more than you think.

Like Rumpelstiltskin, you must convince interviewers you can spin straw into gold for the organization. The purpose of *When Do I Start?* is to launch your campaign to achieve past master status, a title given to medieval artisans who "passed" their exams to become virtuoso craftsmen.

To sum up, I encapsule ten ways to score in the interview and become *a past master.*

1. Study self and practice telling your story.
2. Look good.
3. Impress early.
4. Praise the virtues of hard work.
5. Express yourself clearly and with energy.
6. Edit truth to fit the job.
7. Avoid weakness and tout your talents.
8. Introduce at least one fresh idea, technique or approach.
9. Avoid defensiveness by taking the offense.
10. Leave the interviewer uplifted.

.   .   .

> Job competence will be inferred from
> interviewing competence.

.   .   .

AND AFTER

. . .

This is Interview Number 2 for the MPI Marketing Assistant position described on page 115. No matter what you think of the interviewer, assess Pam's qualifications or lack thereof. Would you hire her this time? Of course, a transcription cannot convey presence, nonverbal communication, the meaning in moments of silence or the appearance and enthusiasm of the interviewee. Still, bolstered by the commentary, I believe you can analyze Pam's approach.

Interview	Annotation
[*Pam, neatly dressed, walks up to the interviewer directly, looks him in the eye, smiles and shakes hands firmly.*]	First impression: Appearance, Entrance, Presence
INTERVIEWER: My name is Paul, I'd rather go on that basis. Please sit down. What do you prefer to be called?	

	Interview	**Annotation**
PAMELA:	I sign myself Pamela. I notice you have a number of books by English authors on your shelf. Perhaps you're familiar with *Pamela*?	Openers: Relevance-raising

Finding common ground for communicating |
I:	Yes, wasn't that an eighteenth-century novel by Henry Fielding?	
P:	Richardson.	
I:	Oh, yes. Fielding wrote *Tom Jones*.	
P:	Right. He also wrote a takeoff on *Pamela* called . . .	
I:	*Shamela*.	
P:	Yes. [*Laughter*]	Jump-starting
I:	I notice you're an English major. Have you read Richardson much?	
P:	I've read *Pamela*, of course.	
I:	Did they require *Clarissa* also?	
P:	I have not read *Clarissa*.	
I:	Lucky you. What about our	

Interview	Annotation

situation that partic-
ularly intrigued you,
fascinated you . . . ?

P: The job description
was quite wide-rang-
ing for the title of as-   Demonstrating
sistant. It seemed to   flexibility
me I would have a
chance to assist in all
areas of marketing,
and hopefully have
an opportunity to ad-
vance in any of a
number of directions.

   The communica-   Highlighting to
tions among a number   the job descrip-
of different depart-   tion
ments particularly in-
terest me, staying in
touch with the product
managers and com-
municating between
them and the direct
sales personnel.

I: Without going into
great detail, could
you give me an ap-
preciation for what
you do in a regular
day from nine to
five?

P: Well, we publish   Team person

Interview	Annotation
about eight hundred titles a year. Between my assistant and myself we publicize those.	"We"
Publicity, one way of looking at it, is unpaid advertising — primarily review in professional journals. I might add, none of our books have been banned in Boston so far. [*Laughter*]	Humor
We try to get author interviews or feature articles on the book.	

I: How do you go about doing this sort of thing?

P: By making up an individual mailing list for each of our books, at least we do. A trade house might automatically send a copy of every book they publish to a list of three hundred and add on to it. Our books are rather specialized, so we make up an individual list for each

	Specific, to the point

Interview

Annotation

one. And we also pre-
pare a certain amount
of publicity material
for almost every book,
and a substantial
amount for eighty or
ninety titles a year.

I: Excuse me, does this
mean press releases,
blurbs, etc.?

P: For the most part, yes.
All the marketing de-
partments work pretty
closely together, and
we feel free to *canni-
balize* from each oth-
er's copy. So I'm
very pleased when our
releases end up in li-
brarians' newsletters
or jacket copy or di-
rect mail pieces. It's a
question of figuring
out what will sell a
book. I guess it's that
analytic part of mar-
keting that appeals to
me—how will it benefit
the customer?

I: Okay, I'm going to go
back into your past
for a bit—I have a

Tiger word

Creativity

Interview	Annotation
feel for what you're doing now. Tell me about yourself.	
P: Actually my family moved around a lot. I went to high school in Wakefield, Virginia. I think that's where Robin Hood was from—not Virginia, of course.	Homework on self
	Drawing a tangent
I: Right, Wakefield, England.	
P: I graduated from Wellesley College. . . .	
I: Yes, I notice in English with high honors. Why English? What fascinated you about that, or was it simply the shortest line at registration?	
P: No, my parents instilled a love of reading in me, and English is something you can enjoy all your life as an avocation. I particularly like writing. I'm a good writer, a fast writer, and that's been obviously helpful to	Solid family background
	Self-confidence

Interview	Annotation
me in my job. Also in my community activi- ties. I've done articles for community groups and managed to get them published in *The New York Times* and *Daily News.* I wrote a history of our neigh- borhood that was published.	Good citizen
	Initiative-taker

I: That's great.

     Let's address the time you've been with Felton, Inc., which is a little over two years. Are there one or two things you're most proud of? If someone asked you what you've contributed to the face of the earth over the last two years, other than the oxygen-CO_2 cycle, in your profes- sional life, what would you answer to that?

P: Let's see. [*Pause*] In my publicity respon- sibilities we were able to inspire some front- page stories for our	Pregnant pause

Interview	Annotation
books in *The Wall Street Journal*, which had never been done before. Feature stories rather than book reviews, which means you get a lot of readership that we think is more valuable. It happens we published the first book on zero-based budgeting. It took *hard work* to get a feature article on it, but we were able to do it. We also promoted six other lesser-known books in the same way.	Floy floy, a go-getter
	Work ethic
In terms of the company, I get to work with many departments and see places to improve. Without being a *mad memoist* [*laughter*], I make suggestions I see appropriate. For instance, I recommended a procedure to speed up ordering that was adopted	Picturesque speech
	A do-it-now person

Interview	Annotation
by top management and saved considerable time and money.	Business-minded
I: What sorts of things do you read on your own, other than books you have to write publicity about?	
P: Mysteries [*with a smile*]. I love to try to solve them. And novels—I'm fairly conservative in my fiction tastes.	Problem solver Middle of the road
I: Where would you like to be going—I don't mean this as the usual inane question when people say, "Where do you want to be in five years?" No one really knows that. Where would you like to be going over the short haul, as it were?	
P: The process of marketing fascinates me. I would like to be a marketing director, all right, at some point. And there are	Upward bound

Interview	Annotation
various intermediate steps I could imagine, such as working in advertising or being a product manager.	Slanted to the job description

I: Okay, I think you've answered the question. Getting into a full-fledged marketing operation, there is a requirement for some statistical background. There's nothing in your experience that indicates you could cope with a large quantity of numbers. Have you had any exposure to this sort of thing?

P: Not statistics per se. — Unflappability

I'm a quick study, and if required I would take a course to learn statistics. Felton sent me to a course on finance and, I must confess, I went reluctantly, expecting to be bored, and was surprised how interesting it was, and moreover — Turning a negative into a positive

Interview   **Annotation**

that the different concepts in accounting make sense. Since then I've used those concepts in budgeting our promotion costs.

I: Okay, so you wouldn't have an apoplectic stroke if someone handed you a calculator and said we have to run these figures through, or something like that.

Interviewer likes the explanation

P: No. [*Smiles*]

I: That's good to know because we do have people who would reenact the *Bounty* situation if that were brought up, and we'd have a riot on our hands, and we don't want that. [*Laughter*] The job is not heavily statistically oriented, but there is some of it in there.

Interviewer is feeling good

In your present position you have some supervisory responsibility. How

Interview	Annotation
many people are you supervising now?	
P: My position is more coordination and liaison, but I have an assistant and half a clerk.	Slanted to the job description
I: Half a clerk, that must be tricky.	Humor
P: Yes. [*Laughter*]	
I: How do you get them to do the things that need to be done?	
P: Um, I'm still learning. With the clerk, she's an older woman, I found the most important thing that made us work together well was to explain why I was asking her to do a task. Inevitably much of the work is extremely dull and repetitive but must be done accurately. Just helping her see where that tedious job fits in to achieve our goal helped make it a more palatable job.	Open-minded

Leadership

Good with people |

	Interview	**Annotation**
I:	What would you say, if you had to catalog your virtues, are your strongest points?	
P:	In a business setting, you mean.	Humor
I:	Yes, yes, sorry I should have said that. [*Laughter*] If you had to fall back on one or two skills to accomplish your business objectives, what would they be?	
P:	I think I'm very conscientious and hard-working, and I have a certain amount of flair and imagination to analyze a situation and propose a plan for it.	Well-stated summary of self
I:	Okay, good. There is one question I would want to ask you. If you had the entire realm of recorded history to choose from, who would you want to spend a day with?	

Interview	Annotation
P: Oh, wow. For an imagined list, it would be fascinating to know anyone who has created an enormous world of very living people—Shakespeare is the obvious one.	Answering the unexpected
I: Okay, that's about all the questions I have.	
P: I'd like to ask a few. I have some understanding of your business. I read the annual report and talked to the manager of a store that sells MPI products. But this particular job, what's the key quality you're looking for?	Close: Homework on the organization Cross-question
I: I'd say it's marketing savvy first, working with people second, and third being able to coordinate promotion and budgeting.	
P: Well, I'm very interested in the job and excited about it. The salary is within my	Outline your position

Interview	Annotation

expectations. I be-
lieve my background
in promotions and
publicity, working
with several different
departments, has
provided me with the
experience to be a
marketing assistant.

I'd like to leave you with this copy of a plan I developed for marketing one of our most successful books.	Leave some thing of value
I: Thank you, I appreciate that, and I'll look it over.	
P: What are the next steps, as you see them?	Seek commitment to next steps
I: I have three more people to see, but I'm very interested in you. I'll be back to you within two weeks.	
P: I appreciate that, because I'm considering two other offers.	Not overanxious
I: If you need to know before two weeks, call me. Don't take another job without	Sign of encouragement

Interview	**Annotation**
calling first. Okay?	
P: Okay, sounds fair enough. I want you to know I really enjoyed the interview. Not all of them are this interesting.	Kudos to the interviewer
I: I enjoyed it too, and I appreciate you coming in. We'll be talking with you the week after next.	
P: Thank you. [*Shaking hands*]	
I: Take care.	

POSTSCRIPT: Pam connected with the interviewer. She was offered the job.

APPENDICES

. . .

Appendix A. EEO (Equal Employment Opportunity) Considerations

. . .

What Is It?

A number of laws and executive orders have led to what is called Equal Employment Opportunity (EEO), including:

- The Equal Pay Act of 1963
- The Civil Rights Act, Title VII, 1964, and as amended in 1972
- The Age Discrimination in Employment Act of 1967, and as amended in 1978
- The Rehabilitation Act of 1973
- The Vietnam Discharge Act of 1974

In addition, in 1966 President Lyndon Johnson (and other presidents have followed) initiated a series of executive orders

that provided for withholding government contracts to organizations not complying with EEO laws.

Out of this legislation came the Equal Employment Opportunity Commission (EEOC), the federal agency assigned to
oversee discrimination issues.

Applicable to the job market, EEO regulations state that
no organization can deny a person employment because of:

- Race
- Color
- Religion
- Sex
- National Origin
- Age
- Physical Handicap

These seven categories have been the basis for thousands of
EEO class-action suits in the last two decades.

Implications for Interviewing

Certain questions asked in the interview or employment
application could be construed as EEO violations. Here are
some examples:

- What's your marital status?
- If not married, are you living with someone?
- Do you plan on having children?
- How's your credit rating?
- What will your children be doing while you're working?

- What organizations do you belong to (e.g., NOW, NAACP)?
- What kind of discharge did you get from the military?
- How old are you?
- What if your husband is transferred?
- Would it bother you working with an all-male sales force?
- Would it bother you working with whites?
- Do you belong to a church?
- How do you feel about women's lib?
- Do you smoke or drink?
- Have you ever filed a discrimination claim?
- How will your husband feel about your traveling?
- Have you or your children ever been arrested?
- How long a commute do you have?
- How do you feel about homosexuality?
- What is your national heritage?

Note that most of these questions are not illegal per se, but in an investigation, they could be interpreted as discriminatory.

What Does This Mean for You?

If you are asked any of these questions, you must choose to respond or not. If you confront interviewers with, "That's not job related," you will likely be rejected. If you fail to complete similar items on the application, you won't make it to the interview.

If your objective is to find employment rather than make a social statement, I recommend you answer all questions in some fashion. If you find a given question too personal, respond in generalities or divert to a related topic.

EXCEPTION: It is possible, but rare, you will meet an interviewer whose queries are so outrageous that no sane person would take them seriously. Example: A few years ago a Wall Street investment bank was recruiting at Stanford University. The interviewer asked a student, "Would you have an abortion to save your job?" He asked another applicant whether she was "religious" to determine if she was a "good girl" or a "partier."

No way would I respond to that kind of third degree, nor would I work for a company that conducts interviews of that ilk. You are not likely to meet up with such unwitting and terrifying mindlessness. Most incidents of noncompliance with the letter and spirit of EEO are subtle and inconspicuous.

I repeat: *Answer all questions as best you can.* If, subsequently, it becomes clear you did not get a job because of one of the seven discriminators, refer the case to your nearest EEOC office for possible action.

Appendix B. Typical Questions Cross-Referenced to the Nine Principles

• • •

These thirty questions are typical of the ones you will be asked. They may vary according to job level and your experience and education, but the general content is here. I have left out monadic questions with one definite answer (e.g., What school did you attend?) and binary questions requiring only a yes or no (e.g., Did you graduate?).

Practice your responses. To help you I have cross-referenced the thirty to the Principles in this book. If you can handle these, you will experience few surprises in your job search.

		Principles
1.	Tell me about yourself.	1, 2, 5, 6
2.	How has your experience (or education) prepared you for this job?	1, 4

Principles

3. What would you characterize
    as your strengths?   1, 5, 9

4. What would you say is your
    greatest weakness?   4, 5

5. What are your professional
    goals?   1, 7

6. What bores you in work?   5, 7

7. What motivates you?   1, 3, 7

8. Tell me about your greatest
    accomplishment (or proudest
    moment) in the last year.   5

9. What frustrated you most in
    your work this year?   4, 5

10. What was your greatest fail-
    ure (in work or school) and
    what did you learn from it?   4, 5

11. Let me describe a situation;
    you tell me how you would
    handle it.   3, 6, 8

12. What trends do you see for
    our industry?   1, 8, 9

13. Why do you want to work for
    us?   1, 3, 5

14. What do we gain by hiring
    you?   1, 5, 9

15. Why do you want to leave
    your current position?   4, 5

16. Define what you think it takes
    to be a successful manager
    (engineer/salesperson/re-
    searcher/secretary)?   3

Principles

17. What do you like to do most
    in your nonwork hours?   3, 6, 7
18. What have you read lately?   7
19. What distinguishes you from
    others applying for this job? 1, 5, 7, 9
20. What do you know about us?   1, 8, 9
21. Do you have any questions?   8, 9
23. On a 0–10 scale, how would
    you rate yourself as a leader
    (manager/organizer/problem
    solver/creator/coworker)   3, 4, 7
24. When others criticize you,
    how do you feel and react?   3, 5
25. What kind of person do you
    most enjoy working with?
    Least enjoy?   3, 5
26. Describe a typical day in your
    life.   1, 5, 6
27. What is the chief reason you
    think people fail in a job like
    this? Succeed?   3, 5, 7
28. What are your feelings about
    travel/relocation/working
    overtime?   9
29. Who has been most influential
    in your life? Explain.   1, 6
30. How would you describe
    yourself?   3, 4, 5, 6

INDEX

• • •

Index

269